Seasons
of the Heart
and Home

Quilts
for Summer
Days

Jan Patek

American Quilter's Society

P. O. Box 3290 • Paducah, KY 42002-3290

ACKNOWLEDGMENTS

Special thanks to Kathy Cosgrove for calculating the yardage.

All Quilt Photos: Richard Walker, Schenevers, NY.

All Quilts: Designed and constructed by Jan Patek; quilted by Jan Patek, and under her instruction, by Verna Graber.

Library of Congress Cataloging-in-Publication Data

Patek, Jan.
   Quilts for summer days / Jan Patek.
         p.   cm. – (Seasons of the heart & home)
   ISBN 0-89145-818-2 : $18.95
      1. Quilting–Patterns.   2. Patchwork–Patterns.   3. Appliqué–Patterns.
      4. Patek, Jan–Diaries. I. Title.   II Series.
TT835.P385   1993
746.9'7–dc20   93–25842
                                                                        CIP

Additional copies of this book may be ordered from:

American Quilter's Society
P.O. Box 3290
Paducah, KY 42002-3290
@18.95. Add $1.00 for postage and handling.

...quilts are journals in a way to all of us – whether we design our own or not. Maybe that's one reason quilting is so enduring. Through our quilts and the colors we choose, we have made statements about ourselves and what is important to our lives – houses, trees, wedding rings, churns, stars, sunshine, and shadows. No matter what happens we keep on quilting....

TABLE OF CONTENTS

INTRODUCTION

The last three years have been difficult for me. Like so many other women my age, I have been dealing with what are known as Empty Nest Syndrome, Mid-Life Crisis, and Menopause.

During these years I have started keeping a journal and continued making quilts. I make one-of-a-kind, abstract quilts, and I make "quilt" quilts. Most of the pain and turbulence of this period has been expressed in my art quilts. In fact, anyone looking at those quilts from this period of my life will probably say, "My God – that poor woman!"

But there has been a healing side to this time, too, and there have been real rewards on the other side of the turmoil. Healing, I have found, I express best in my "quilt" quilts.

The quilts in this book are very special to me and, if I can keep my children from grabbing them as fast as they're made, I look forward to using them and healing with them for years to come. It is my hope that these selections from my journals and my quilts will add to others' lives as much as they've added to mine.

THE JOURNAL / THE QUILTS

I don't want noise and energy and exuberance for awhile. I want to work on my quilts and lay in the sun and play with my cat. I need the space and warmth of summer right now – and the structure of the repetitive and familiar. They say that nature heals. I notice that most of these quilts are about nature – sun, flowers, trees, chickens, ducks, my cow....

"Patio Pot," 40.5" x 51". See page 34 for pattern.

12 February 92

Snow outside – flowers and sun inside. It's been such a mild winter. Snow in November and then very little cold weather. No more snow until today. I must stop quilting in awhile and make a run to Lexington to pick up Max. Senior pictures of a cadet and his red jeep in the snow....

Working on the flowers is comforting. At this time of year I'm still enjoying the bareness of things. No flowers or vegetables to weed, no grass to cut, the cow doesn't need milking. Especially the grass! "Summer Skies" reminds me of the beginning of summer when the skies are so blue and the flowers are still the softer colors. I want the quilt to have a feeling of spaciousness – big, open, blue skies – soft flowers contained by a white fence.
Soft, mellow colors and feelings....

"Summer Skies," 93" x 105.5". See page 42 for pattern.

1 March 92

"What makes it hard to live in the world is also what makes it easy to
make art, the intense self-examination."
(Lee Malerich, in <u>Celebrating the Stitch: Contemporary Embroidery
of North America</u> by Barbara Lee Smith, ©The Taunton Press,
1991.)

"Placemats," 23" x 16" and 19.5" x 12". See pages 58 and 62 for patterns.

"Sunny Days," 21.5" x 30". See page 60 for pattern.

6 March 92

"Sunshine at my Window" is done. It grew on me like so many of them do. It started out to be a throw for naps on the couch. When it was finished and hanging on the wall, Pep said it reminded him of looking out the window on a sunny spring morning. All right! That's what I wanted it to say. With the last of the kids moving out this winter, I need the gentleness of spring, and sunrise has always been my favorite time of day. When the kids were little, I started getting up early, because I needed some time in the day when it was quiet. Over the years I loved my little bit of space. I would sit in my chair and do handwork and watch the sunrise. It's still my favorite time – something I look forward to. I want this quilt to say that.

And I love my flower placemats. I think I will do some with the cloud and grass and some just with a flower.

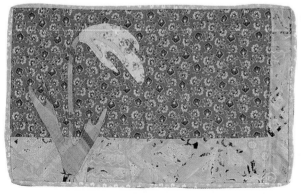 

"Placemats," 19.5" x 12". See page 62 for patterns.

"Sunshine At My Window," 70" x 87". *See page 68 for pattern.*

8 March 92

I am having more trouble making myself a throw for the couch. "Little House" turned into a crib quilt. I looked at it when it was finished, and it said "baby." It commemorates the house that Brian, his father, and his brother built by themselves. Quite an accomplishment when you're only 20. It's small, but it meets his needs while in college. He even built a flowerbed and planted some evergreens.... and now we are "Neighbors."

It's good to have Brian right down the road and Max and Kelly only 45 min. away. They're all far enough away to be independent and yet still close. I know a lot of people have kids clear across the country or even the world, but I'm not ready for that yet, and I'm not sure I ever will be. I wonder how Ruth handles Mark's moving to Japan? I want to see my grandchildren grow up — go to their school programs and ball games. I hope we stay neighbors, but whether they're down the road or across the world, I can always make them quilts. That helps.

"Neighbors," 45" x 28.5". See page 74 for pattern.

12 March 92

This crib quilt thing is growing. I love "Kelly's Bunnies."
For the life of me, I couldn't draw a bunny, so Kelly drew one for
me. I abstracted it a little and then used material from one of her
high school sundresses for the sashing and small borders. Kelly said
"Mom, I'm not ready to have babies!" None of them are, but
grandmas can prepare. I think I'll start looking for cribs at farm
sales and get the cradle back from Doug and Alecia.

"Kelly's Bunnies" or "Little House" would look stupendous draped
over a white iron crib.

"Kelly's Bunnies," 52" x 57". See page 78 for pattern.

19 March 92

It's 4:00 in the morning. The dogs went off at something – a coyote probably. Anyway, lying there I suddenly realized why I make quilts!

My quilts aren't just pretty designs that I think look nice. My quilts are a journal of my life – inside and out. They're a record of what is going on in my life emotionally and literally. They are statements about things that impact me and that I consider important.

I think quilts are journals in a way to all of us – whether we design our own or not. Maybe that's one reason quilting is so enduring. Through our quilts and the colors we choose, we have made statements about ourselves and what is important to our lives – houses, trees, wedding rings, churns, stars, sunshine, and shadows. No matter what happens we keep on quilting.

I'm not at all sure just who I am right now – now that the main part of my mothering job is over. I didn't think that I would have much trouble when my children grew up because I have always had my art. But I am having trouble. I miss them and the vitality they brought to my life. Not enough to start again, though – that part of my life is over. So who am I right now, and what am I doing? I don't know, but I do know that I want to keep on quilting – soft colors and lots of space, lots of warmth and comfort, lots of summer skies.

"Little House," 51" x 68". *See page 84 for pattern.*

21 May 92

Brian is almost 22, Kelly turned 21 on May 19th, and Max is graduating from high school. And I am sometimes not sure that I am going to make it through this transition period. I'm just not sure that there is any way to do this gracefully.

"Little Silkies," 19" x 26". See page 87 for pattern.

10 June 92

Mid-life crisis, empty nest syndrome, and menopause. My – what a threesome! Major sense of loss and tearing – questioning.

Is this all there is? Am I still somebody when the kids leave? I want to spend some time figuring out exactly who. Letting go…. that's hard! Like learning to function without a piece of yourself. Unsettling – feels strange, even "wrong." But part of it fills a deep need for space for me now.

"Baskets & Berries," 20" x 20". See page 88 for pattern.

14 June 92

I really like the beginning of "Summertime" or "House and Tree, Me and Thee, II." I'm not sure what to call it yet – maybe both. Anyway, I used green and purple as my base colors and had no idea why. Then last night as I came in from shutting up the chickens, I realized that green and purple are the colors of summer twilight. The whole world goes green and purple. I can hear the chickens settling and the cicadas singing and watch the lightening bugs flash. Such a feeling of peace and tranquility. Nice feelings for a change. I like them. I'm pretty sure that the vine in the border of the quilt represents my marriage. Look at all those nice blooms! No thorns there right now, thank God.

"Summertime (House and Tree, Me and Thee, II)," 56" x 70". See page 90 for pattern.

12 July 92

I have decided that the log cabin quilt is for Brian's child —
when it is a child, not a baby. I want the duck that Brian drew and
stitched when he was eight to be passed on to his child when it is
eight. "...an individual life can appear isolated and without purpose
unless recognized as contributing continuity to lives that precede it
and follow it, endowing each human span with rich universality."
(Turn: The Journal of an Artist, Anne Truitt*) That feeling of
continuity is very important to me right now. I can let my boy
become a man and my daughter become a woman as I prepare
quilts for their children.

*From Turn: The Journal of an Artist by Anne Truitt. Copyright 1986 by Anne Truitt.
Used by permission of Viking Penguin, a division of Penguin Books USA Inc.

"Brian's Duck Sampler," 10" x 9". See page 114 for pattern.

14 July 92

The flowers of my quilt look faded and mellow, like I'm feeling.
I don't want noise and energy and exuberance for awhile. I want to
work on my quilts and lay in the sun and play with my cat. I need
the space and warmth of summer right now — and the structure of the
repetitive and familiar. They say that nature heals.
I notice that most of these quilts are about nature — sun, flowers,
trees, chickens, ducks, my cow....

"Log Cabin," 70" x 90". See page 116 for pattern.

17 August 92

I miss my Maxwell. He moved into the dorm two days ago, and the house is strangely quiet. Everything is a double-edged sword these days. Each step of independence they make, which gives the parent in me feelings of relief and satisfaction, also brings feelings of loss and sadness.

"Young Man's Fancy," 88" x 95.5". See page 123 for pattern.

23 August 92

"Young Man's Fancy" – made for Brenda Lawler (Brian's girlfriend) is my interpretation of who she is and who she can be. I must like her. I think maybe this quilt is part me, too. As a mother with three teenagers, I've needed a backbone of steel just to maintain some sense of control in the house. Three whirlwinds don't leave much room for softness. With them tucked safely away in college, I can breathe again. I can stop and re-explore the pastel shades of myself.

"Young Man's Fancy (small)," 28" x 34.5". See page 130 for pattern.

16 September 92

Miss Katrina is sitting on my lap and Jo-Jo's asleep at my feet. I'm quilting "Empty Baskets" as I wait for the sunrise. A few years ago I would have put something in the baskets. Now I have decided to leave them empty. Full baskets mean that the harvest is in progress. Nancy came over Monday and needed two gallons of tomatoes for picante sauce. Take them!! Take all you want! The pantry is full, and we'll just need a few tomatoes for eating and for the vegetable soup we'll can this week. Everything is in except the gourds and the pumpkins. Even the "Baskets in the Garden" are empty.

I think that the empty baskets symbolize something else for me, too. My days are no longer filled with the flurry and scurry of children. At first that was painful – the emptiness. Now its beginning to be exciting. Empty baskets mean that the days are mine to fill. There's time for myself, my husband, time to play with my Silkies and baby swan. There's energy for the flowers – not just the vegetables and grass.

I wonder what my quilts will look like now? I can tell by "Patio Pot" and "Summertime" that my need for pale and mellow is ending for now. Fall is here and my mind starts filling with different colors – deep oranges, greens and golds, sumac reds…. I haven't made Max his graduation quilt – that definitely needs to be red….

And Christmas with primitive angels and Santas. And lots and lots of houses and trees. Home is very important....

"Empty Baskets," 17.5" x 26.5". See page 134 for pattern.

"Baskets In The Garden," 61.5" x 79". See page 136 for pattern.

PROJECTS & PATTERNS SECTION

Complete patterns and instructions for making the quilts and placemats pictured with journal entries are included in this section, occasionally with slight changes in overall measurements for easy use of instructions. Keep the following in mind as you work with the patterns and instructions:

(+sa) = plus seam allowance. All patterns pieces and measurements need to have ¼" seam allowance added. The lines given in the patterns are sewing lines, not cutting lines.

Borders – As each of us sews a little differently, I would suggest measuring your quilt before cutting the borders for which I have given you measurements. Most of the time, I am sure that we will agree but occasionally....

Patterns – Keep in mind that these are folk-style patterns, which have a very personal style to them. I encourage you to use the patterns and my quilts' layouts as a starting place. Relax, experiment, and have fun creating your own version of each quilt. Add a second cat to the design if you have two! Include your son as well!

As this is a pattern book and, therefore, general instructions for appliqué, piecing, and quilting techniques are not included, you may want to consult your favorite publications for assistance in these areas. The following books available from AQS (toll-free 1-800-626-5420) would also be helpful:

For general techniques:
From Basics to Binding by Karen Kay Buckley
Quiltmaker's Guide by Carol Doak
Classic Basket Quilts by Marianne Fons & Elizabeth Porter

For appliqué:
My Mother Taught Me to Sew by Faye Anderson
The Art of Appliqué by Laura Lee Fritz

For quilting:
The Ins and Outs: Perfecting the Quilting Stitch by Patricia Morris
Quilting with Style by Gwen Marston & Joe Cunningham

PATIO POT
40" x 50" finished size

FABRIC REQUIREMENTS
Center and outer border
   ¾ yd of dark
   ½ yd of medium
   ⅝ yd of light
   ¼ yd of gold for inner border,
      flowers and vase accents
   ½ yd of red plaid for 2nd border
      and vase
   ¼ yd of red print for flowers
      and berries
   ½ yd green for stems and leaves

INSTRUCTIONS (Patterns pages 37-41)
   • Piece background according to Diagram #1
   • Cut and piece bias strip of green 114" x 1"
   • Press under edges – finished strip will be 114" x ½"
   • Cut and piece bias strip of green 76" x ½"
   • Press under edges – finished strip will be 76" x ¼"
   • Position bias for stems and vines. (I pin in place and sew later.)
   • Cut vase, leaves, flowers, and berries and appliqué into place according to
      Diagram #2 or referring to photo.
   • Cut 2 gold borders 28" x 1" (+sa)
   • Cut 2 gold borders 40" x 1" (+sa)
   • Sew 28" x 1" borders to top and bottom
   • Sew 40" x 1" borders to sides
   • Cut 2 red plaid borders 40" x 1" (+sa)
   • Cut 2 red plaid borders 32" x 1" (+sa)
   • Sew 40" x 1" borders to sides
   • Sew 32" x 1" borders to top and bottom

- Piece outside borders if desired
- Cut 2 borders 32" x 4" (+sa)
- Cut 2 borders 50" x 4" (+sa)
- Sew 32" x 4" borders to top and bottom
- Sew 50" x 4" borders to sides
- Quilt and bind

Diagram #1

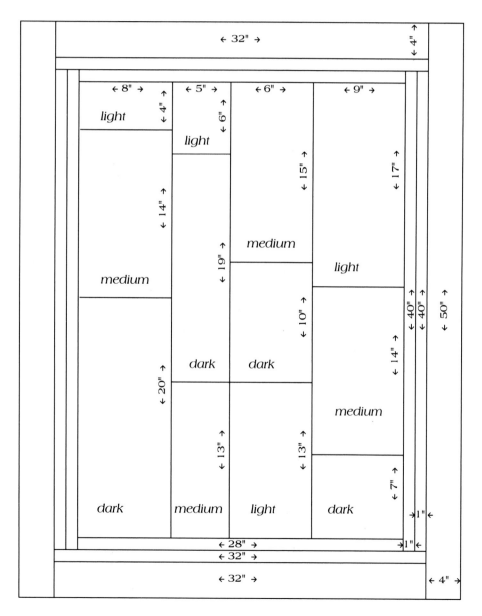

Diagram #2

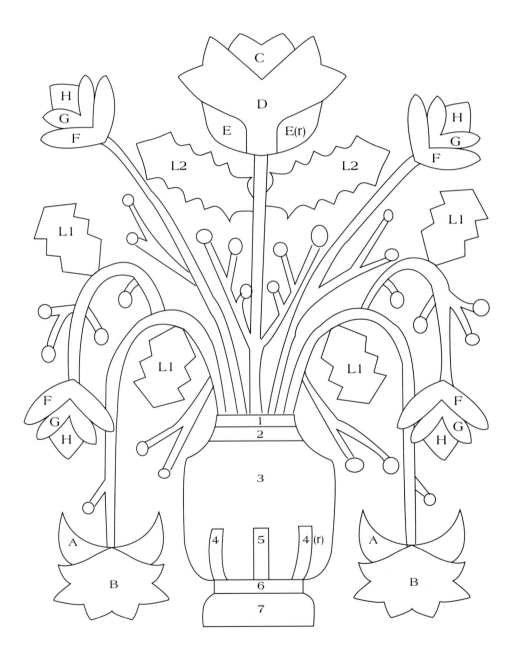

Note: Bias strips are used for stems and vines.

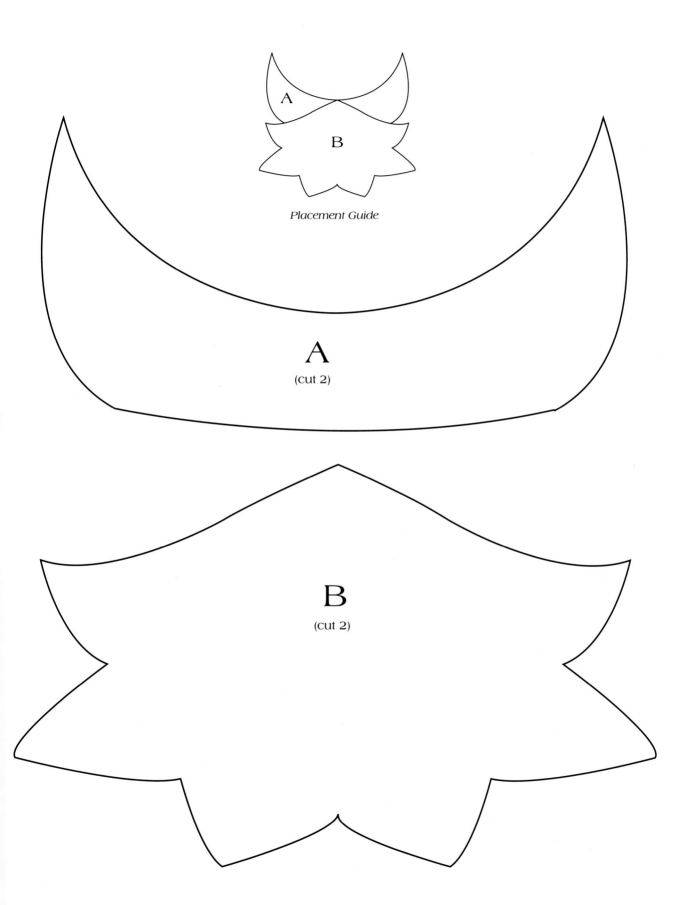

Placement Guide

A
(cut 2)

B
(cut 2)

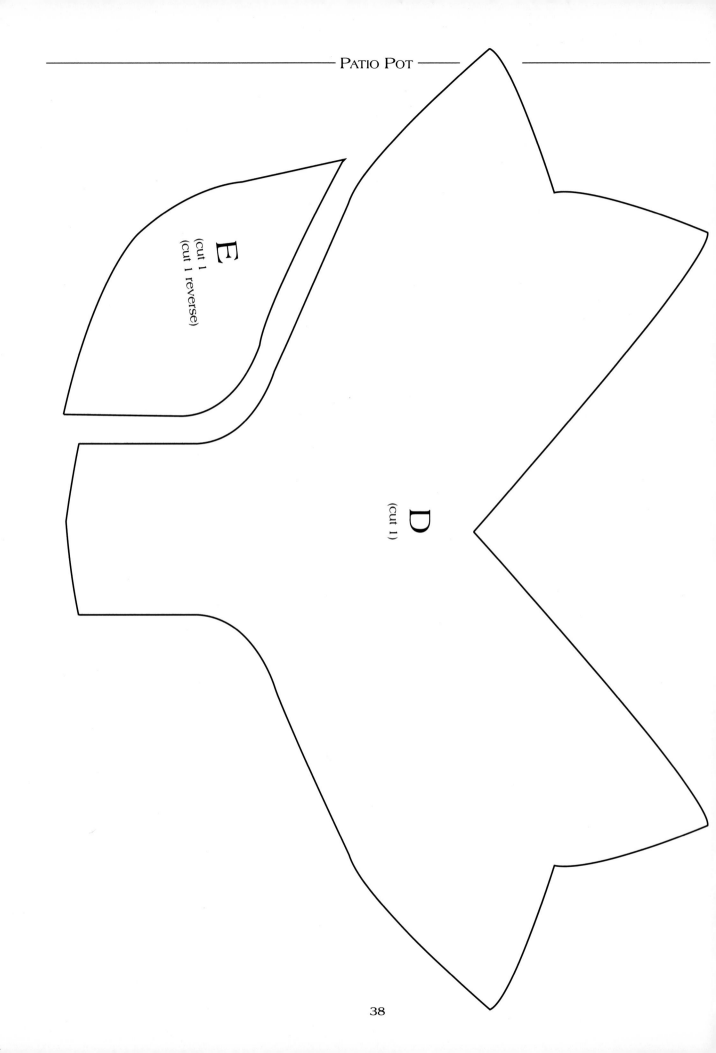

E
(cut 1
(cut 1 reverse)

D
(cut 1)

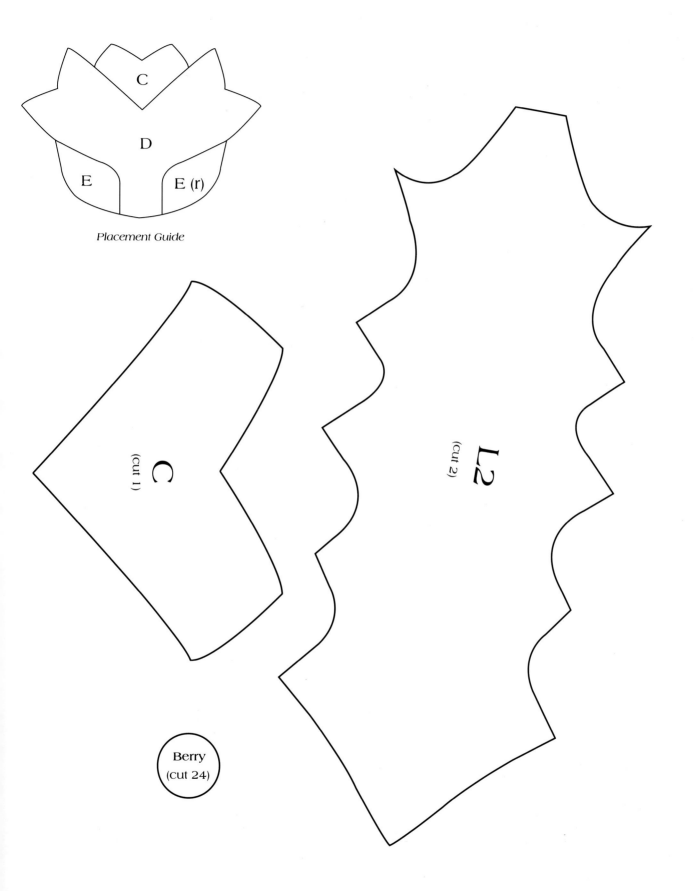

Placement Guide

C
(cut 1)

L2
(cut 2)

Berry
(cut 24)

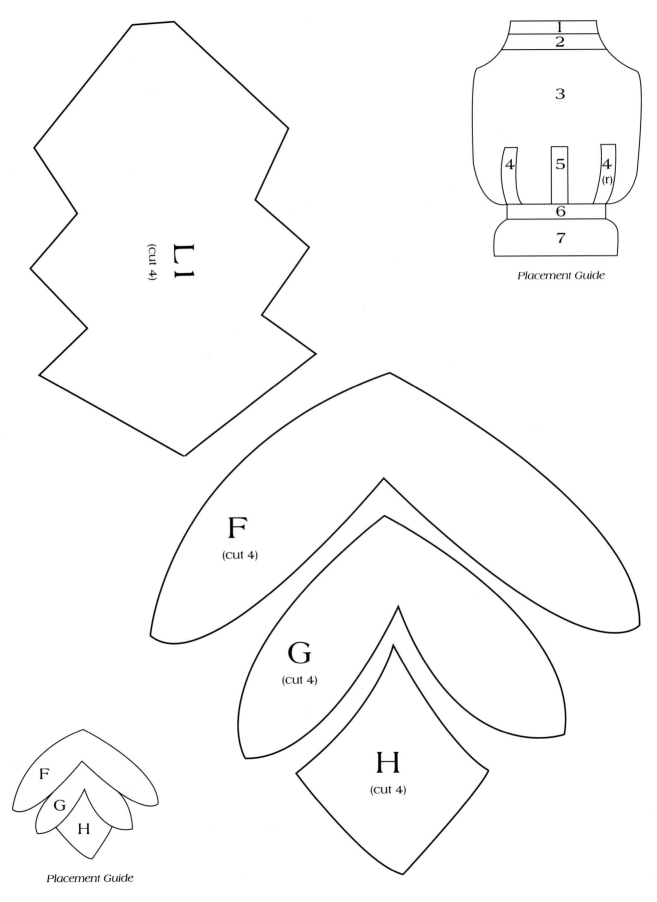

L1
(cut 4)

1
2

3

4   5   4
(r)

6
7

Placement Guide

F
(cut 4)

G
(cut 4)

H
(cut 4)

F
G
H

Placement Guide

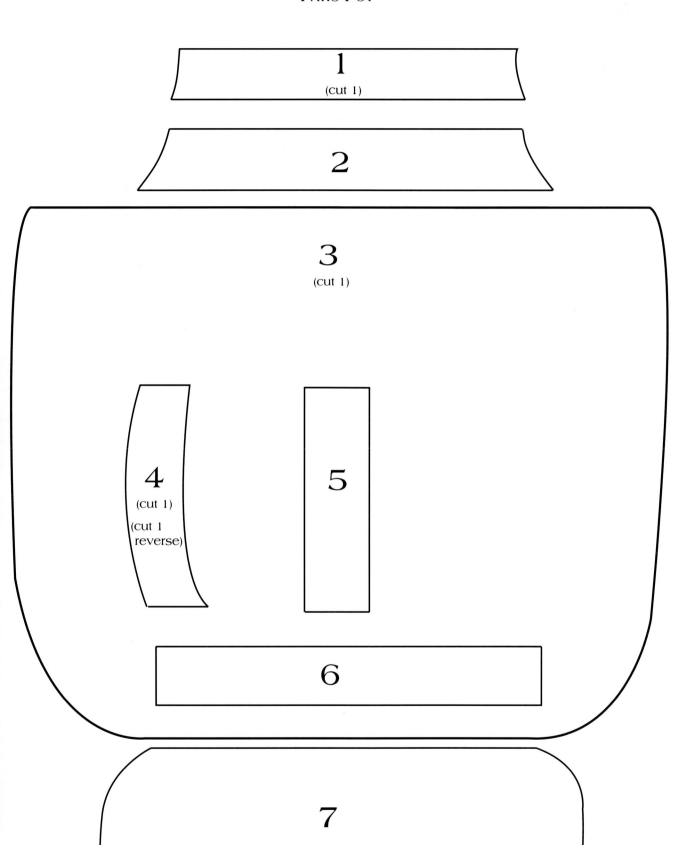

1
(cut 1)

2

3
(cut 1)

4
(cut 1)
(cut 1
reverse)

5

6

7

SUMMER SKIES
92" x 106½" finished size

FABRIC REQUIREMENTS
Flower blocks
  2⅛ yds of blue or
  16 assorted 12½" blocks
Background blocks
  1½ yds of blue-grey
Pastel Triangles
  1¼ yds
Off-white plaid for lattice strips & borders
  ⅞ yds for 36 lattice strips
  1 yd for 600" of lattice strips
  ⅛ yd for 80" x 1" border
  ⅛ yd for 99½" x 1" border
Outside Border
  1⅜ yds of blue print
Assorted scraps for flowers

INSTRUCTIONS (Patterns: pages 44-56)
- Piece background according to *Diagram #1*
- Cut 13 – 12" (+sa) blue squares
- Cut 3 – 12" (+sa) squares of 3 different blue prints
- Cut 15 – 12" (+sa) blue-gray squares
- Cut 18 triangles (piece #1, pattern on page 140) of multicolored pastel print
- Cut 36 – 12" x 2" (+sa) lattice strips of off-white plaid
- Cut approximately 600" of 2" (+sa) lattice stripping of off-white plaid. Sew ends together.
- Cut 4 Corner Set lattice strips (piece #2) of off-white plaid
- Cut 4 each of 12 flowers in assorted pastels
- Appliqué flowers onto blue squares – 16 blocks with 3 flowers each – there are 4 designs, and you need 4 blocks of each design
- Sew triangles (piece #1), flower blocks, and blue-gray squares together with 12" x 2" (+sa) lattice strips in rows, as seen in *Diagram #1*
- Sew together 4 Corner Sets (piece #1, piece #2, piece #1) as seen in *Diagram #1* (only 1 Corner Set is shown – repeat until you have 4 and rotate to fit each corner)
- Sew together Rows 4 & 5 along with top left and bottom right Corner Sets and with 2" (+sa) lattice stripping as seen in *Diagram #2*

- Sew together Rows 1-3 and 6, 7 along with bottom left and top right Corner Sets as seen in *Diagram #2* with 2" (+sa) lattice stripping
- Cut 2 borders 80" x 1" (+sa) of off-white plaid
- Cut 2 borders 100½" x 1" (+sa) of off-white plaid
- Sew 80" x 1" (+sa) borders to top and bottom
- Sew 100½" x 1" (+sa) borders to sides
- Cut 2 borders 100½" x 5" (+sa) of blue print
- Cut 2 borders 92" x 3" (+sa) of blue print
- Sew 100½" x 5" (+sa) borders to sides
- Sew 92" x 3" borders to top and bottom *Diagram #4* (page 57)
- Quilt and bind

Diagram #1

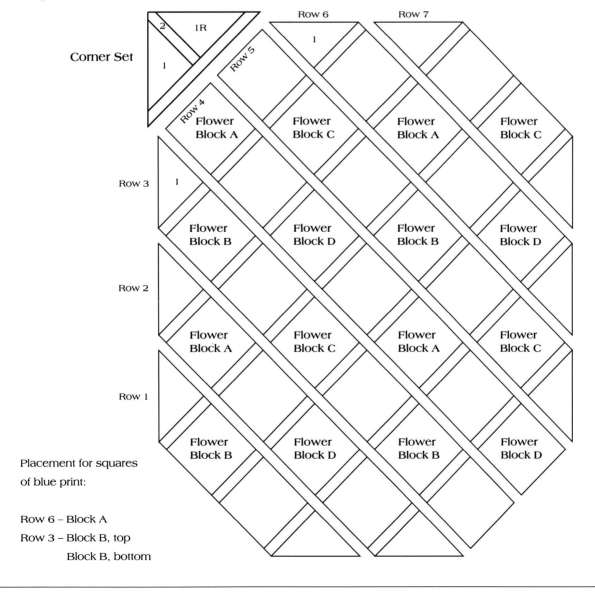

Corner Set

Row 6   Row 7

Row 5

Row 4

Row 3

Row 2

Row 1

Placement for squares
of blue print:

Row 6 – Block A
Row 3 – Block B, top
       Block B, bottom

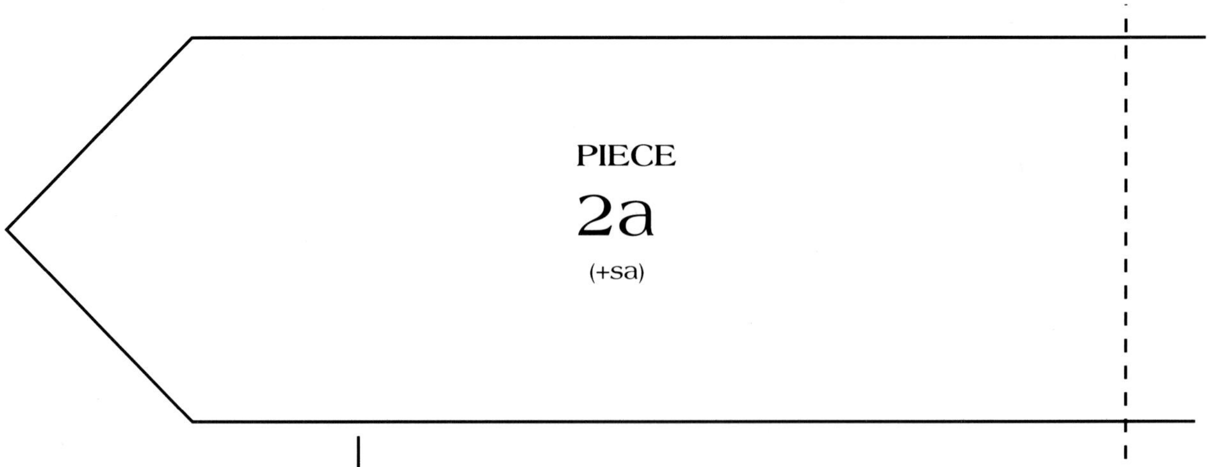

PIECE

2a

(+sa)

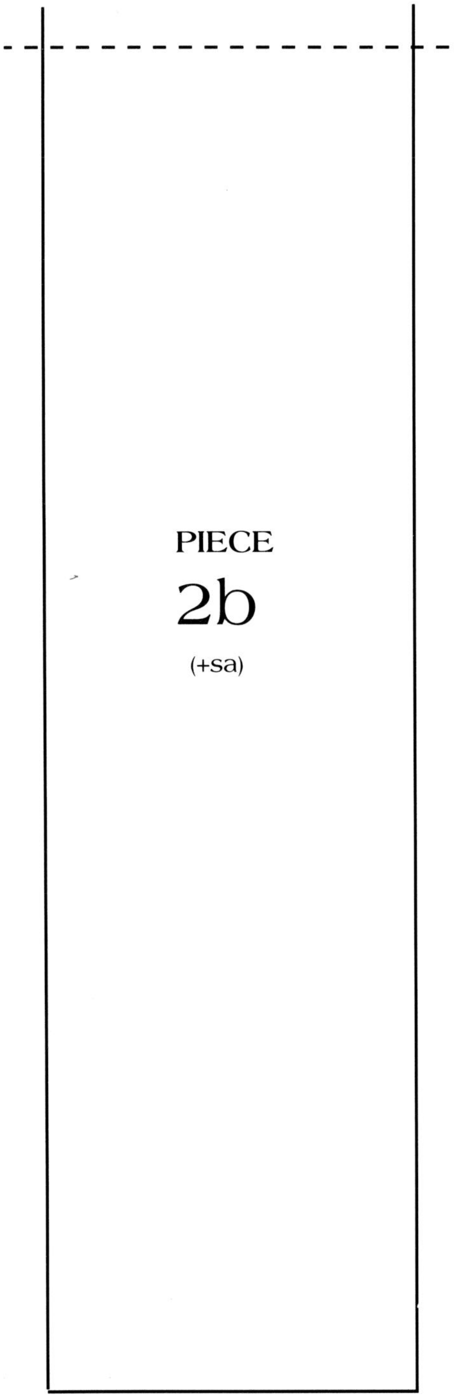

PIECE

2b

(+sa)

Diagram #2

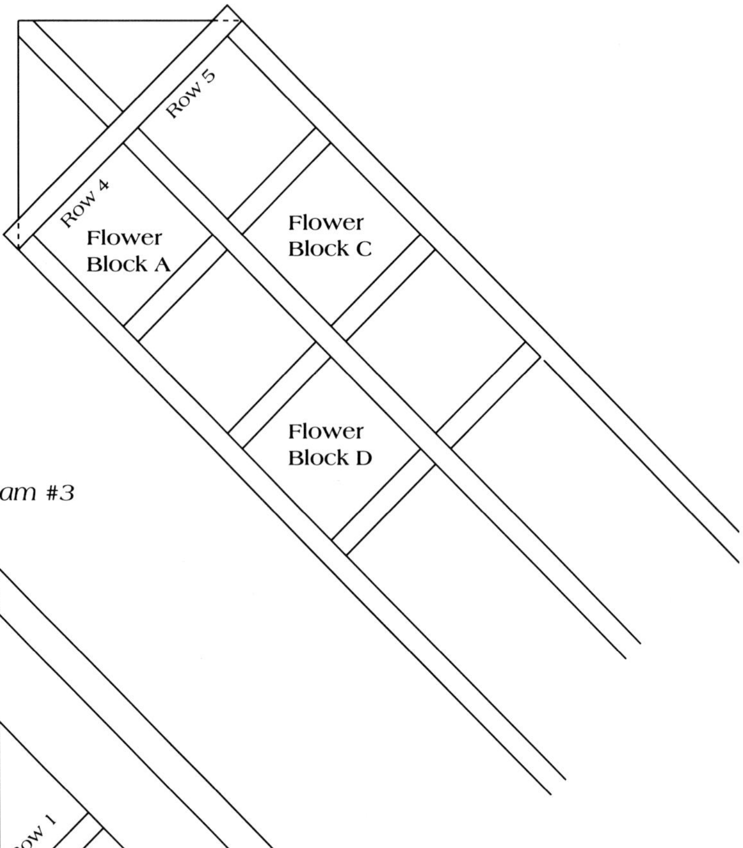

Row 5

Row 4

Flower
Block A

Flower
Block C

Flower
Block D

Diagram #3

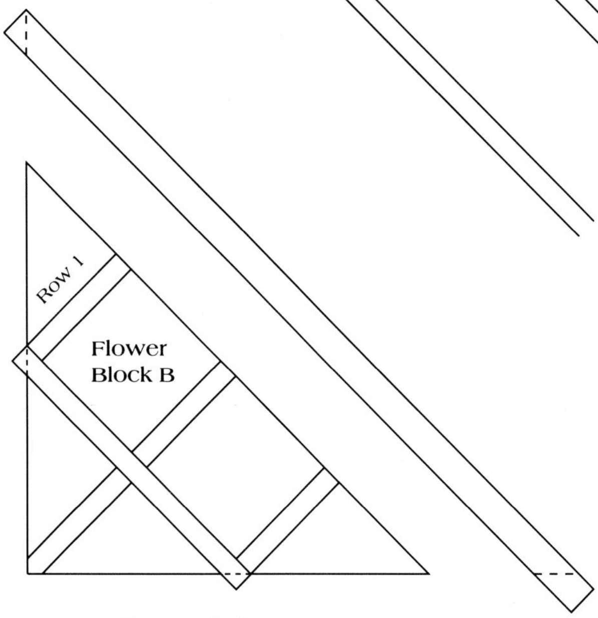

Row 1

Flower
Block B

Corner Set

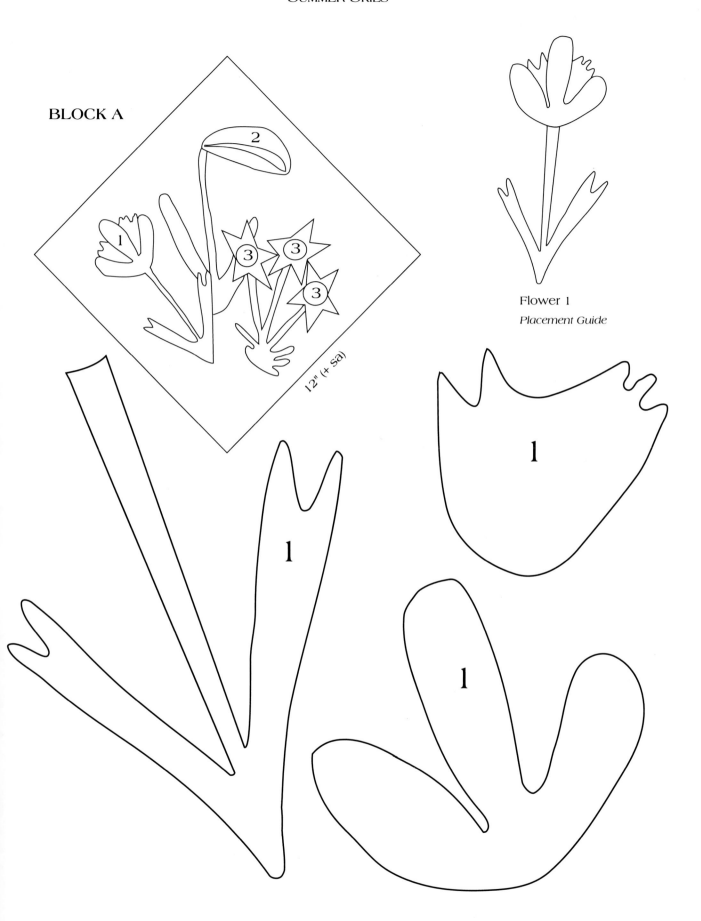

BLOCK A

2

1

3 3

3

12" (+ sa)

Flower 1
Placement Guide

1

1

1

1

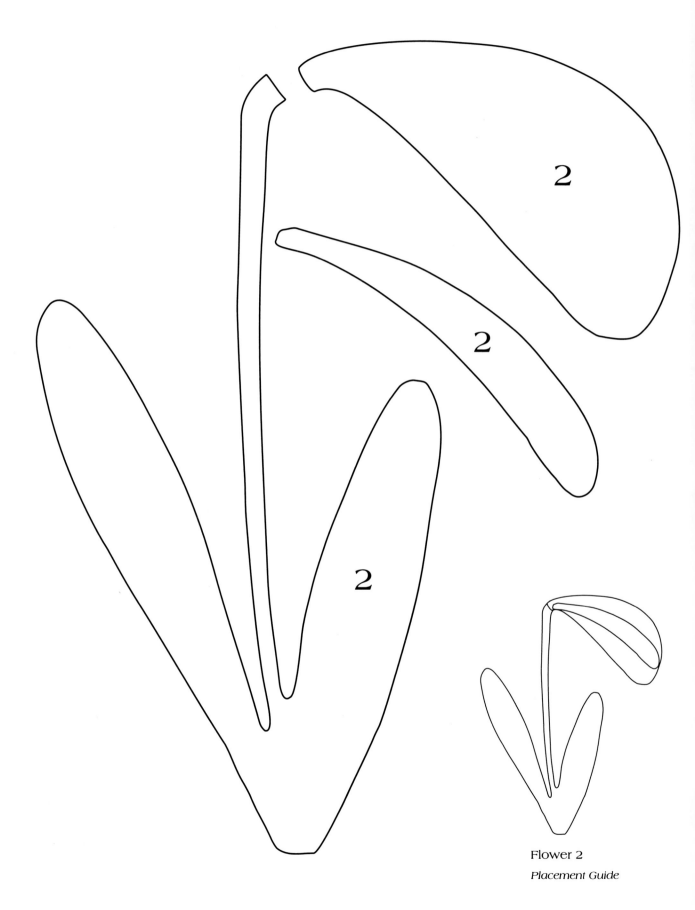

Flower 2

Placement Guide

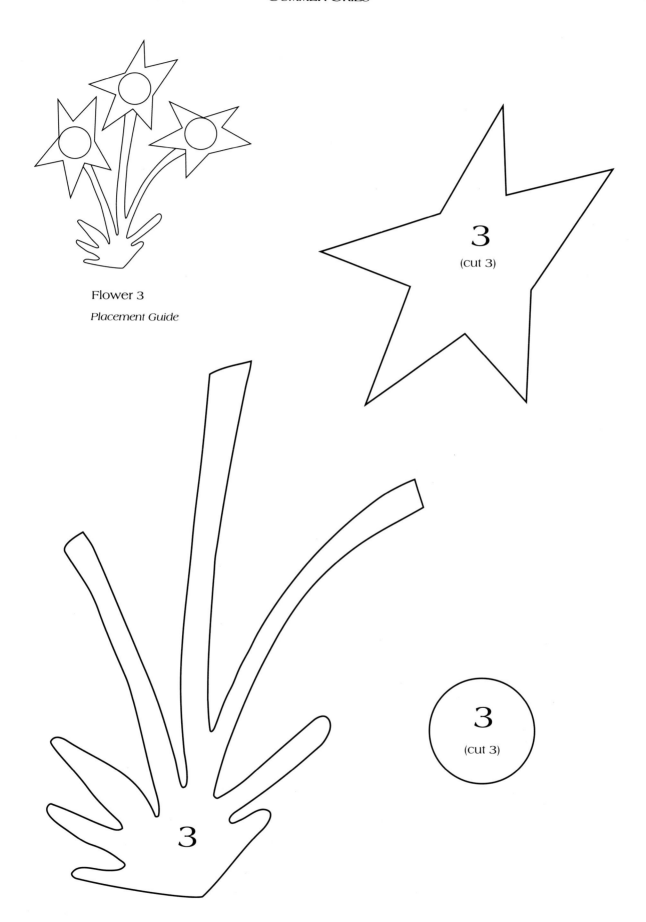

Flower 3

Placement Guide

3
(cut 3)

3

3
(cut 3)

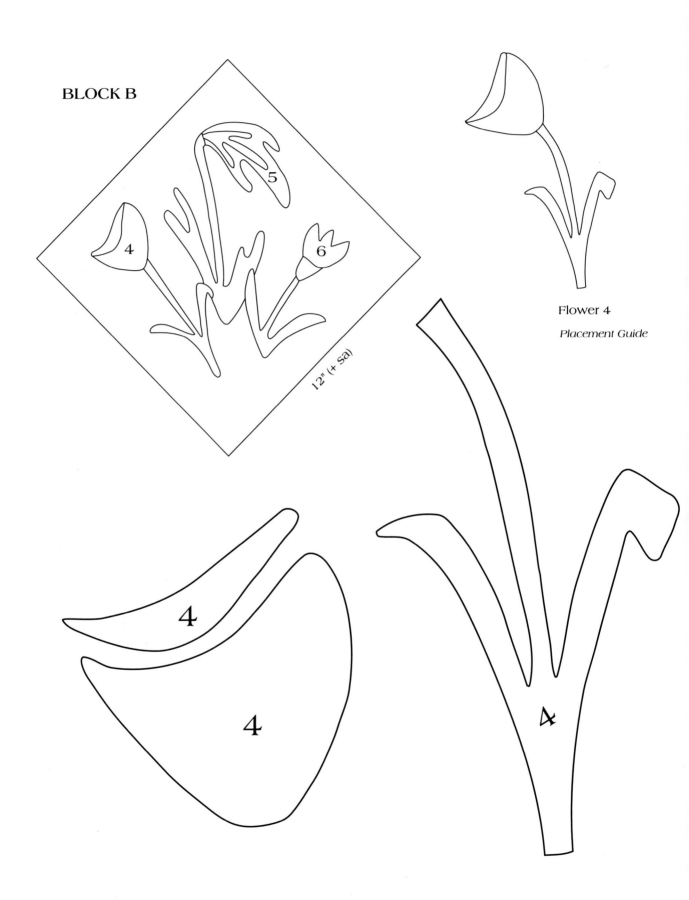

BLOCK B

5

4

6

12" (+ sa)

Flower 4

Placement Guide

4

4

4

5

5

5

Flower 5

Placement Guide

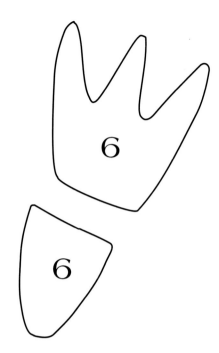

Flower 6

Placement Guide

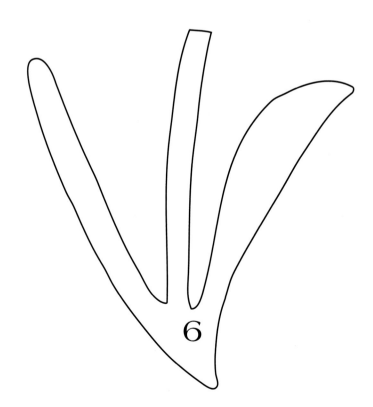

BLOCK C

7

8

9

12" (+ Sa)

Flower 7

Placement Guide

7

7

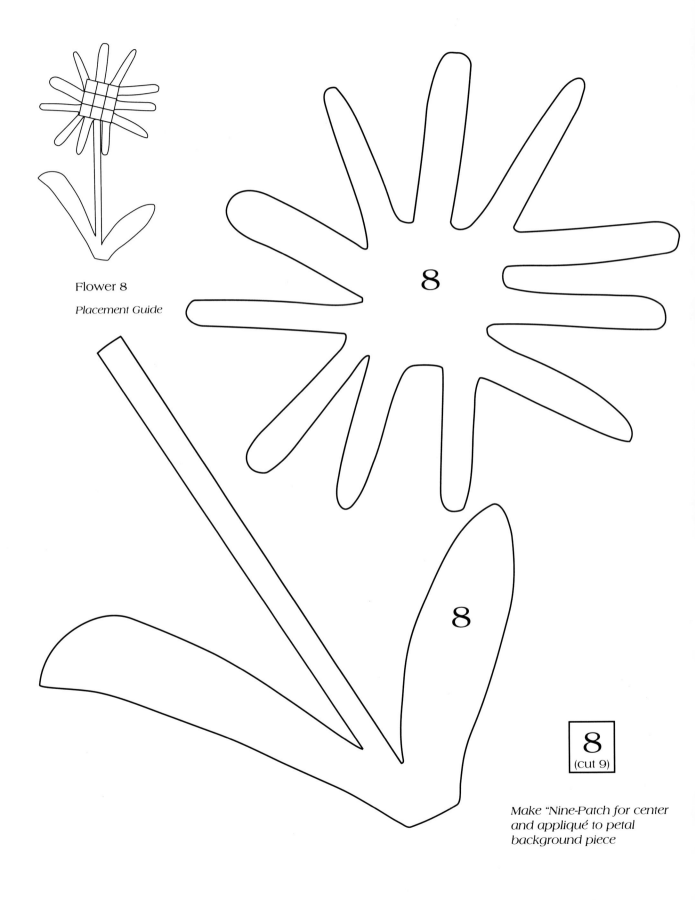

Flower 8

Placement Guide

8

8

8
(cut 9)

Make "Nine-Patch for center and appliqué to petal background piece

Flower 9

Placement Guide

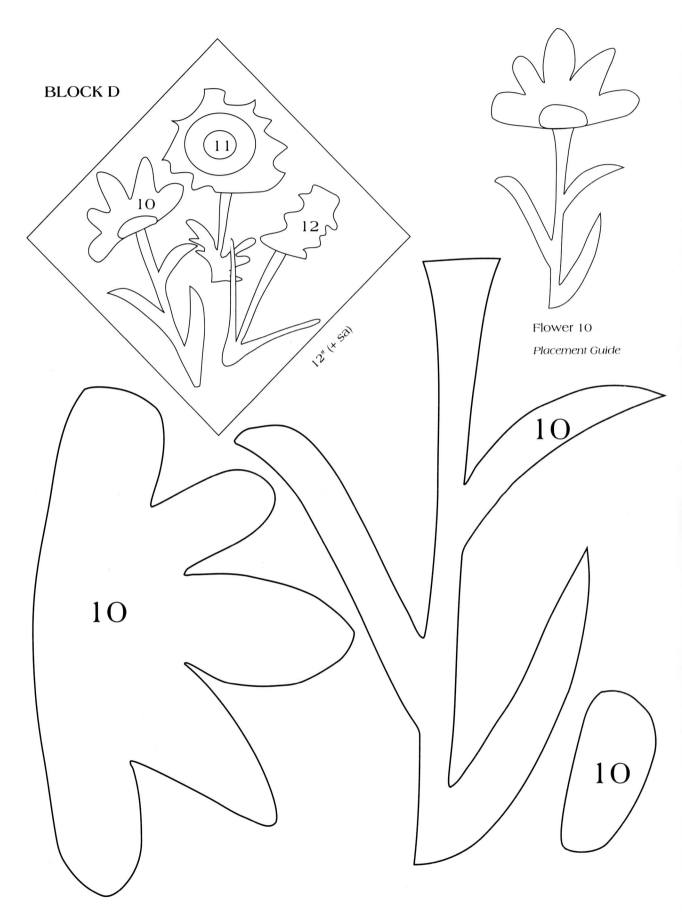

BLOCK D

11

10

12

12" (+ sa)

Flower 10

Placement Guide

10

10

10

10

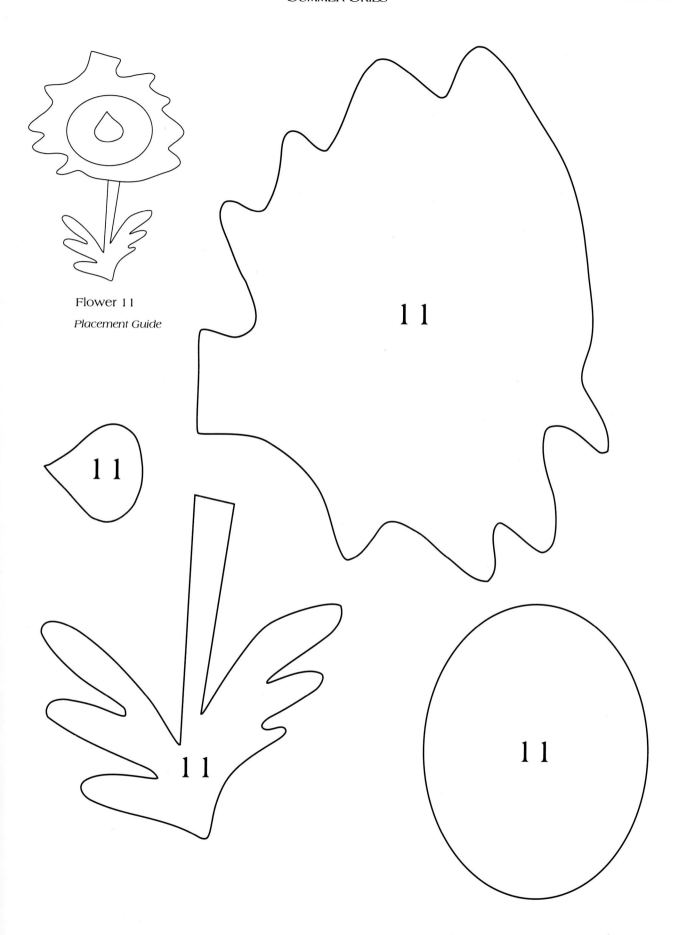

Flower 11

Placement Guide

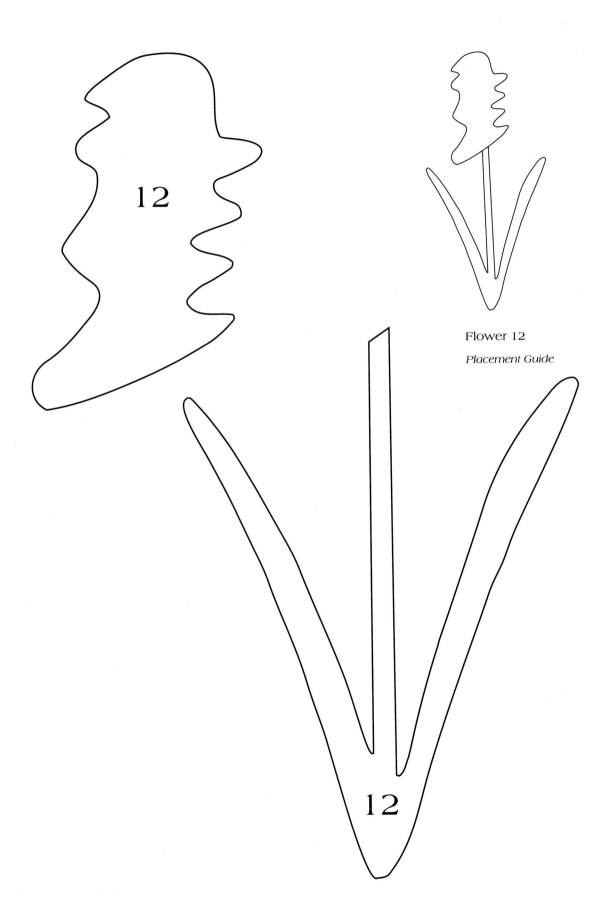

12

Flower 12

Placement Guide

12

Diagram #4

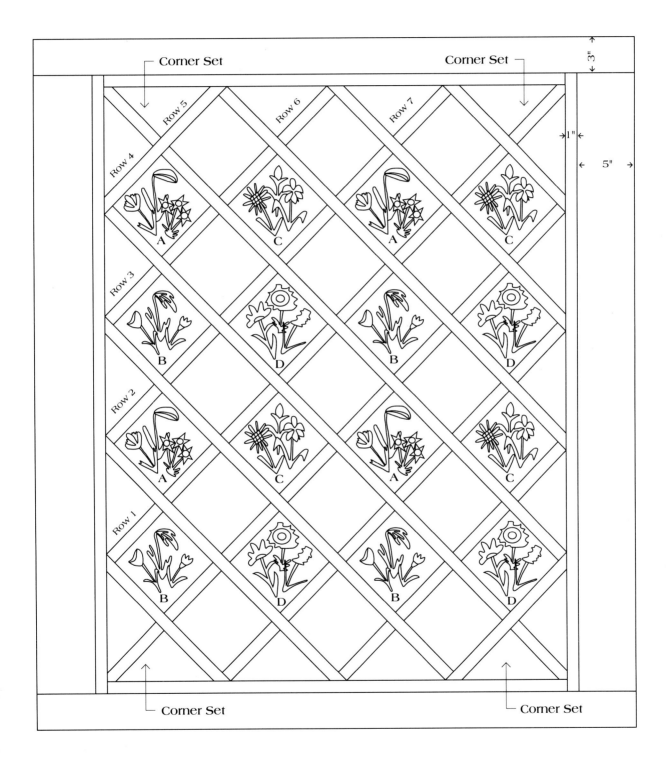

Suzie Cow

Suzie is a Guernsey, big and very gentle, I've been milking her by hand, morning and night for around six years. She comes when she's called, goes to her stall, and stands quietly while I get gallons of rich creamy milk. We do separate most of the cream off. The cats and dogs love us. Milking is a very pleasant, even if demanding, experience. No matter how rushed things are, they slow down and de-stress twice a day.

Silkies are a breed of chickens about half the size of regular chickens. They are all white and have long silky feathers that flow and pouf – I guess that's why they're called Silkies. They have feathers down their legs and on their feet, as well as the regular places. When they're standing still, they look like they don't have legs or feet.

I got some this spring and my husband built them a tiny little house of their own.

ANIMAL PLACEMATS
23" x 16" finished size

FABRIC REQUIREMENTS
⅓ yd for background
⅛ yd for inner border
¼ yd for outer border
Scraps for animals and tree

INSTRUCTIONS (Patterns: pages 60-61, 143-145, 149, 156-157)

- Cut backgound section 17" x 10"
- Cut 2 – 17" x ½" (+sa) borders
- Cut 2 – 11" x ½" (+sa) borders
- Sew 17" x ½" borders to top and bottom
- Sew 11" x ½" borders to sides
- Cut 2 – 11" x 2½" (+sa) borders
- Cut 2 – 23" x 2½" (+sa) borders
- Sew 11" x 2½" borders to sides
- Sew 23" x 2½" borders to top and bottom
- Cut 1 cow, 1 blossoming tree, 1 mama duck, 1 baby duck, 1 reverse baby duck, 1 rooster, 1 mama Silky, and 1 baby Silky (Junior)
- Appliqué the animals and tree in place referring to the photo

I used a buttonhole or blanket stitch to outline the ducks to make them stand out from the background. You may do this if necessary.

See Additional Patterns Section for these patterns:

Page 143   Page 144-5   Page 156   Page 157   Page 157   Page 149

SUNNY DAYS

21.5" x 26" finished size

FABRIC REQUIREMENTS

    ½ yd total for background blocks (or 6 assorted 8" squares)

    ¼ yd for circles or assorted scraps (3 pink and 3 yellow)

    ¼ yd for inner sun or assorted scraps (3 pink or coral and 3 yellow)

    ¼ yd for sashing

    ¼ yd for borders

    ¼ yd for binding

INSTRUCTIONS (Patterns: pages 150-151)
- Cut 3 – 7½" (+sa) squares of white and pastel plaid
- Cut 3 – 7½" (+sa) squares of blue and white stripe or floral
- Cut 3 pink circles (Piece 2)
- Cut 3 yellow circles (Piece 2)
- Cut 3 pink or coral suns (Piece 1)
- Cut 3 yellow suns (Piece 1)
- Appliqué yellow suns to pink circles
- Appliqué pink or coral suns to yellow circles
- Appliqué yellow circles to plaid squares and pink circles to blue squares
- Cut 3 – 7½" x 1" (+sa) plaid sashing
- Row 1 – Plaid square, sashing, blue square
- Row 2 – Blue square, sashing, plaid square
- Row 3 – Plaid square, sashing, blue square
- Cut 2 – 16" x 1" (+sa) plaid sashing
- Join Rows 1, 2, & 3 using 16" x 1" sashing
- Cut 2 – 16" x ¾" (+sa) plaid sashing
- Cut 2 – 26" x ¾" (+sa) plaid sashing
- Sew 16" x ¾" sashing to top and bottom
- Sew 26" x ¾" sashing to sides
- Cut 2 – 26" x 2" (+sa) borders of green floral
- Cut 2 – 21½" x 2" (+sa) borders of green floral
- Sew 26" x 2" borders to sides
- Sew 21½" x 2" borders to top and bottom

See Additional Patterns Section for these patterns:

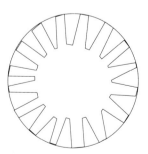

Page 150-1

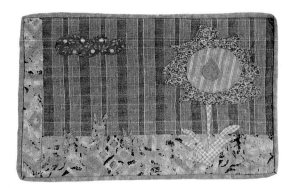

FLOWER PLACEMATS
19.5" x 12" finished size

FABRIC REQUIREMENTS
¼ yd for background
⅛ yd for borders
Scraps for flowers, cloud
and grass

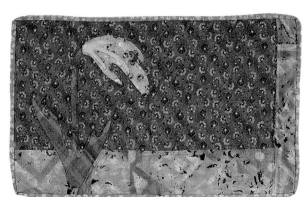

INSTRUCTIONS (Patterns: pages 63-67)
- Cut a 18" x 9" (+sa) backgound
- Cut a 18" x 3" (+sa) border
- Sew these together with border on bottom
- Cut a 12" x 1½" (+sa) border
- Sew this border to either the right or left side referring to the photo
- Cut 3 flowers, 1 cloud and 3 grasses
- Appliqué in place referring to the photo
- Bind

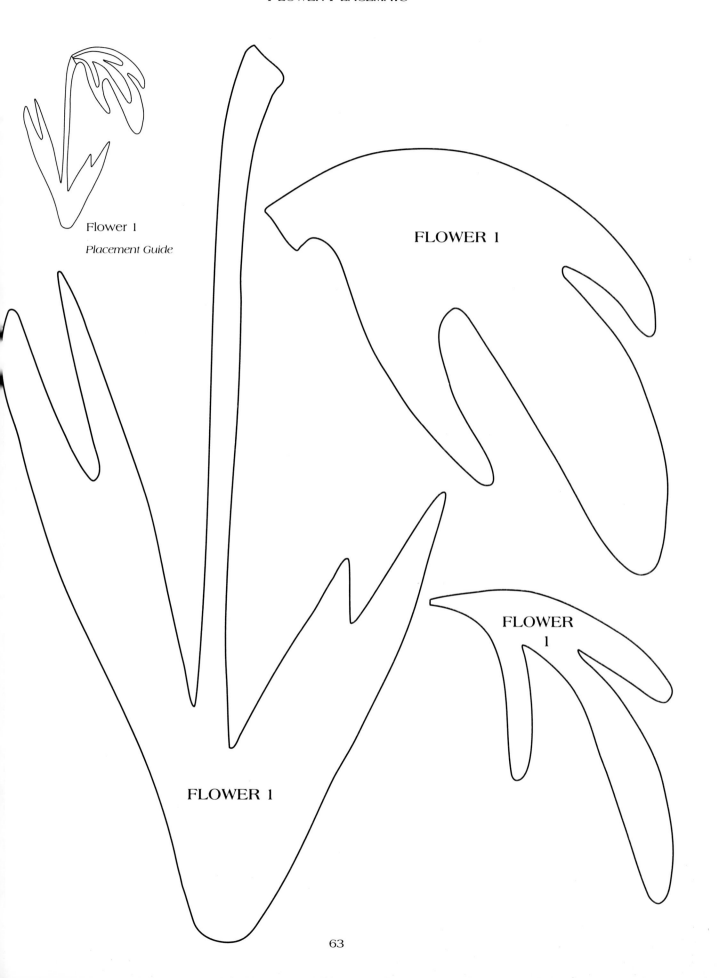

Flower 1

Placement Guide

FLOWER 1

FLOWER 1

FLOWER
1

FLOWER 1

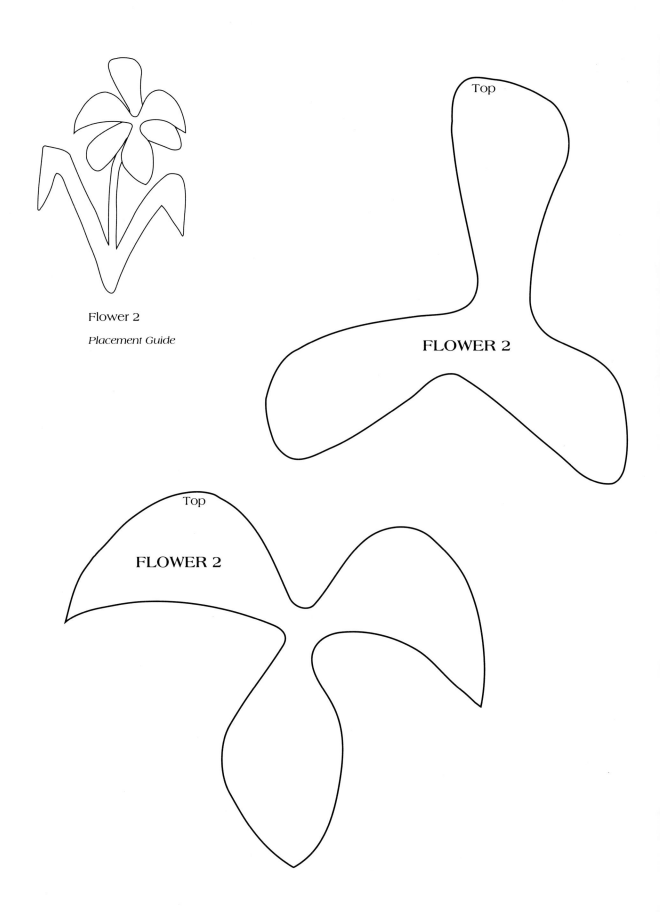

Flower 2

Placement Guide

FLOWER 2

Top

FLOWER 2

Top

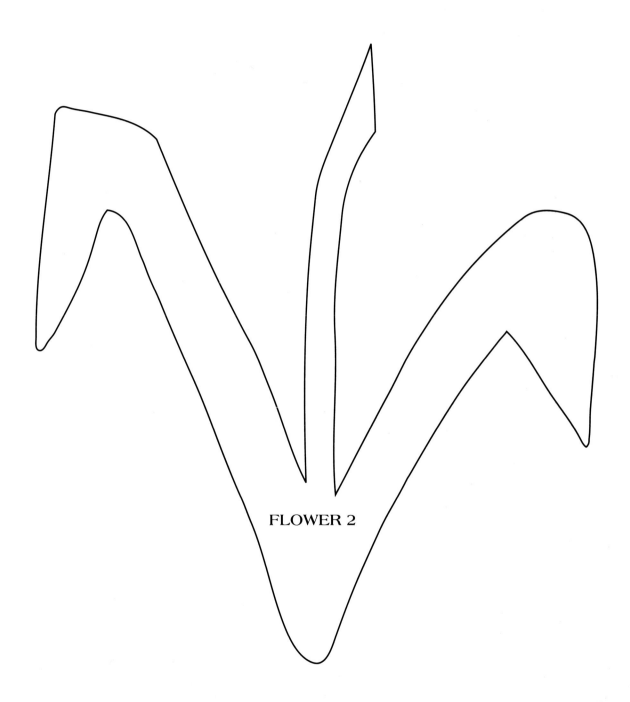

FLOWER 2

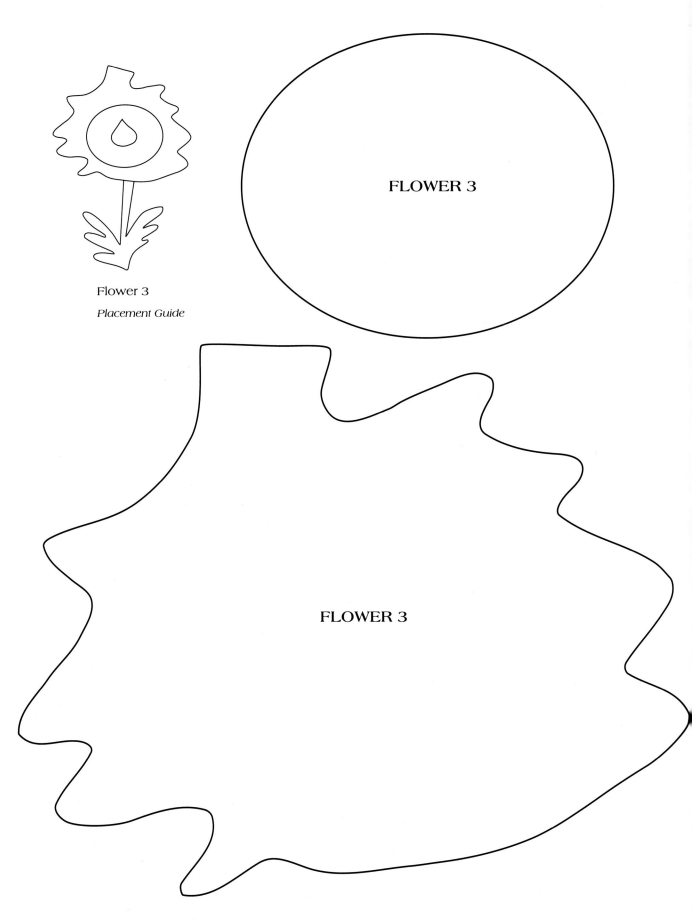

Flower 3

Placement Guide

FLOWER 3

FLOWER 3

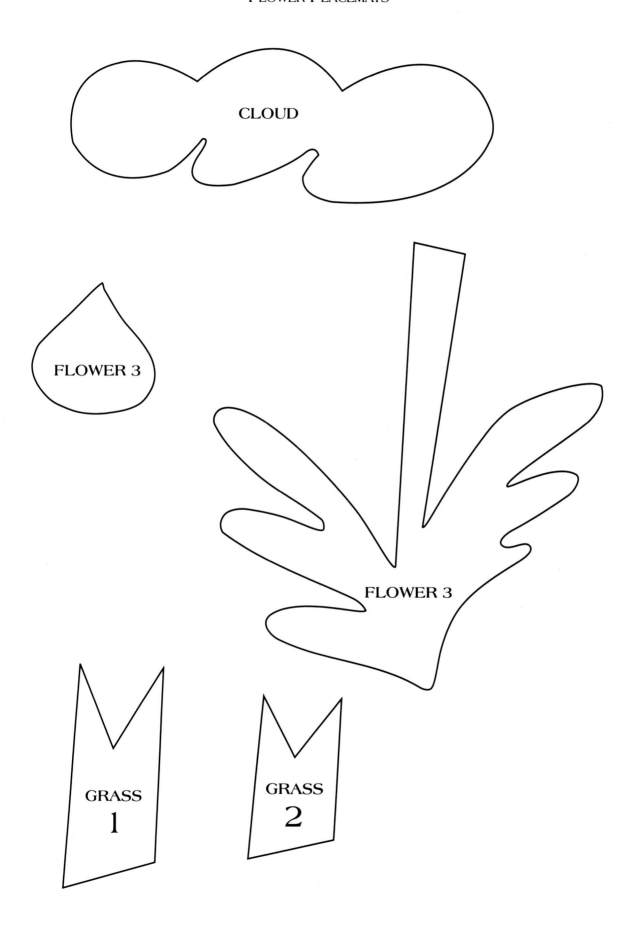

CLOUD

FLOWER 3

FLOWER 3

GRASS
1

GRASS
2

SUNSHINE AT MY WINDOW
69¾" x 87" finished size

FABRIC REQUIREMENTS

¼ yd of 4 colors per sun (each sun is made of 4 New York Beauty blocks –
I have used peaches, corals and yellows)

¼ yd per sun of background colors
(if you use only 1 color for background you need 3 yds of background color)

1 yd of green print for lattices and 1st border

¼ yd muslin for small 2nd border

1 yd of medium green for outside border & corner blocks

½ yd of light green for outside border & corner blocks

INSTRUCTIONS (Patterns: pages 70-71)

- Cut 48 New York Beauty blocks using the templates on p. 70.
- Piece the blocks, as shown in *Diagram 1*.
- Using *Diagrams 2, 3, & 4* as a guide, assemble the blocks (¼ suns) into 1, 2, and 4 piece blocks as required (See *Diagram 5*)
- Cut 8 – 8" x 1¼" (+sa) lattice strips
- Cut 8 – 16" x 1¼" (+sa) lattice strips
- Using *Diagram 5* as a guide assemble strips and suns into Rows 1, 2, 3, & 4
- Cut 5 – 69" x 1¼" (+sa) lattice strips
- Join Rows 1-4 with 69" x 1¼" lattice strips
- Sew 69" x 1¼" lattice strip to each side
- Cut 2 – 54¼" x 1¼" (+sa) lattice strips
- Sew 54¼" x 1¼" lattice strips to top and bottom
- Cut 2 – 54¼" x ¾" (+sa) muslin borders
- Cut 2 – 73" x ¾" (+sa) muslin borders
- Sew 54¼" x ¾" borders to top and bottom
- Sew 73" x ¾" borders to sides

OUTSIDE BORDERS*

- Cut 4 – 73" x 2½" (+sa) medium green border strips
- Cut 2 – 73" x 2" (+sa) light green border strips
- Sew 2 – 73" x 7" (+sa) borders consisting of 1 medium green border strip, 1 light green border strip, 1 medium green border strip
- Sew 73" x 7" borders to sides
- Cut 4 – 55¾" x 2½" (+sa) medium green border strips
- cut 2 – 55¾" x 2" (+sa) light green border strips
- Make 2 – 55¾" x 7" (+sa) borders consisting of 1 medium green border strip, 1 light green border strip, 1 medium green border strip
- Using the patterns on page 72, cut 4 A's, 4 Reverse A's
- Cut 4 B's, 4 Reverse B's
- Cut 4 C's, 4 Reverse C's
- Piecing sequence
- A,B,C,
- AR, BR, CR
- Join to form 4 Corner Blocks as seen in *Diagram 6*
- Sew 1 Corner Block to each end of both 55¾" x 7" borders
- Sew to top and bottom of quilt
- Quilt and bind

Outer borders can also be cut longer and mitered. For that method, omit pattern on page 72.

Diagram #1

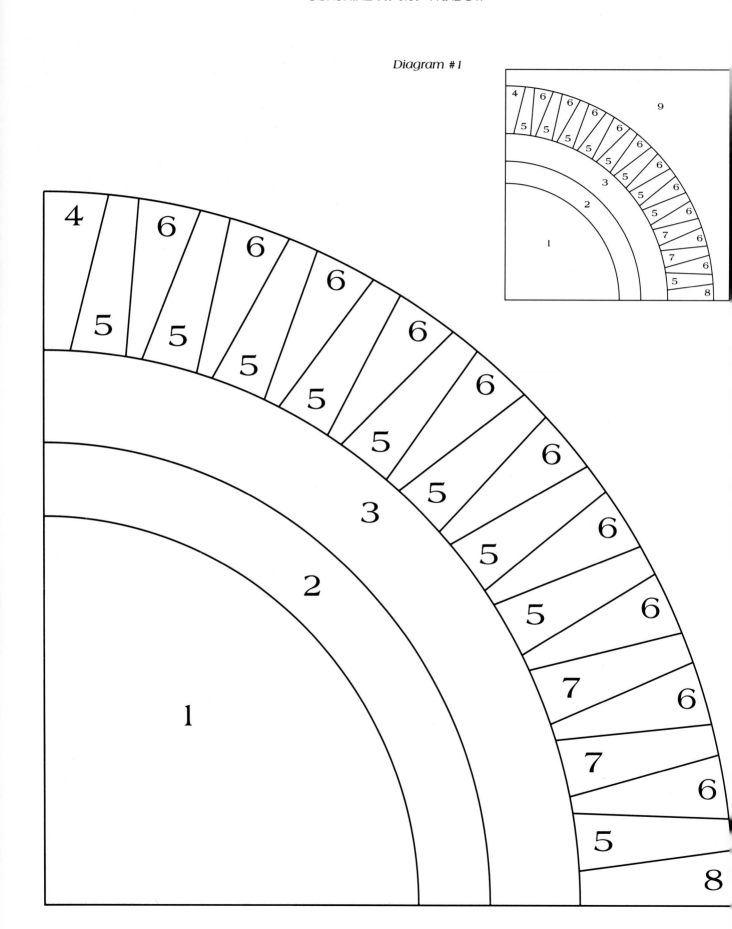

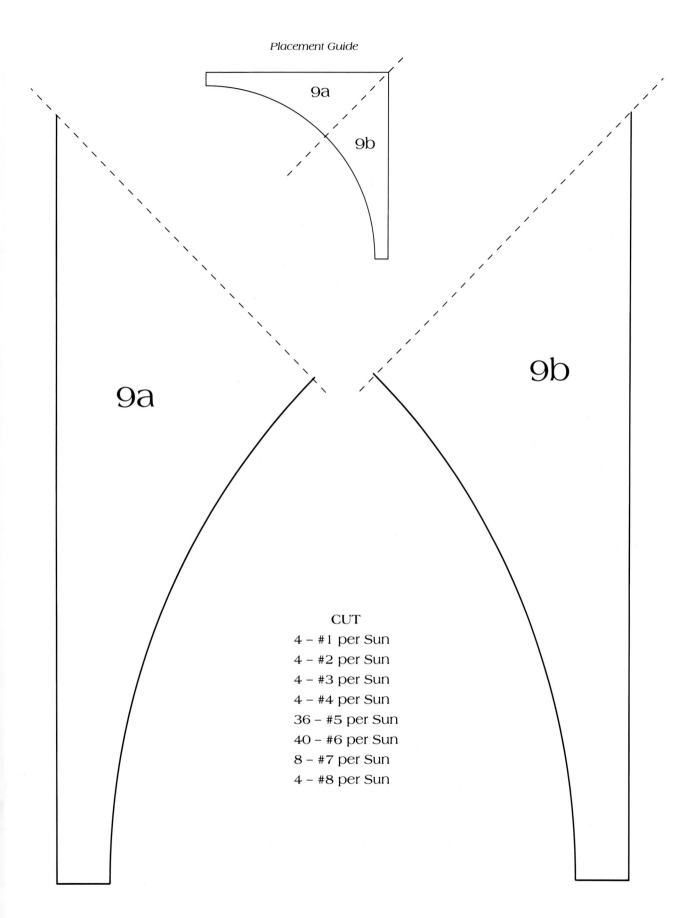

Placement Guide

9a

9a

9b

9b

CUT
4 – #1 per Sun
4 – #2 per Sun
4 – #3 per Sun
4 – #4 per Sun
36 – #5 per Sun
40 – #6 per Sun
8 – #7 per Sun
4 – #8 per Sun

Diagram #5

Diagram #2

Diagram #3

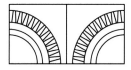

Diagram #4

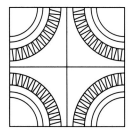

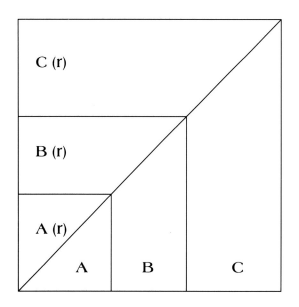

Row 1   Row 2   Row 3   Row 4

Diagram #6

C (r)

B (r)

A (r)

A   B   C

CORNER SET

Full Quilt Diagram

NEIGHBORS

46" x 29" finished size

FABRIC REQUIREMENTS

    Background block for houses ⅜ yd
    Triangles – ⅜ yd
    Small border – ¼ yd
    Large border – ½ yd
    Houses – ¼ yd
    Scraps for trees, grass, flower, sun

INSTRUCTIONS (Patterns: pages 76-77, 144-145, 150-154)

- Cut 2 – 12" (+sa) squares of blue stripe
- Cut 2 triangles (Piece #1) of off-white plaid
- Cut 4 corner triangles (Piece #2) of off-white plaid
- Cut 1 house and 1 reverse house of off-white wide stripe
- Cut 1 roof and 1 reverse roof of lavender print
- Cut 2 windows and 2 reverse windows of gold print

- Cut 1 door and 1 reverse door of gold print
- Appliqué roof, windows and doors to houses
- Appliqué house to blue stripe square set as diamond (See quilt)
- Sew together triangles and squares to make center of quilt
- Cut 2 – 17" x 2" (+sa) borders of blue print
- Cut 2 – 38" x 2" (+sa) borders of blue print
- Sew 17" x 2" borders to side
- Sew 38" x 2" borders to top and bottom
- Cut 2 – 38" x 4" (+sa) borders of off white plaid
- Cut 2 – 29" x 4" (+sa) borders of off white plaid
- Sew 38" x 4" borders to top and bottom
- Sew 29" x 4" borders to sides
- Cut 3 blossoming trees (Tree A) of pink and coral with green trunks
- Cut 1 cherry tree (Tree B) with green trunk and coral cherries
- Cut 3 crocuses of lavender and yellow with blue stems and leaves
- Cut 1 background circle from "Sunny Days" of pink plaid
- Cut 1 sun from "Sunny Days" of yellow
- Cut 9 pieces of grass of green prints, plaids, and stripes
- Appliqué sun onto background circle
- Appliqué trees, crocuses, sun, and grass in place according to photo

I originally appliquéd the houses onto the squares at a really weird angle. They looked like they were sliding downhill. As I already had the backs cut out, I took them off, appliquéd them to a small square of material and appliquéd this small square to the larger one. Voila! Houses on solid ground, and I like the way the quilt looks. If you like the same look, I would suggest appliquéing the houses to a smaller square to begin with (probably with the stripe going in a different direction than the stripe in the large square). You will have enough left over material from the background block yardage to do this if you wish.

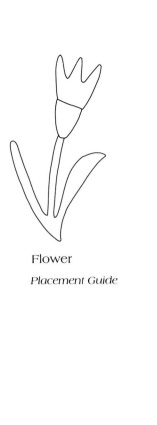

Flower

Placement Guide

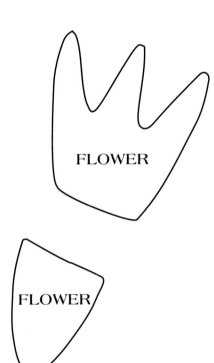

FLOWER

FLOWER

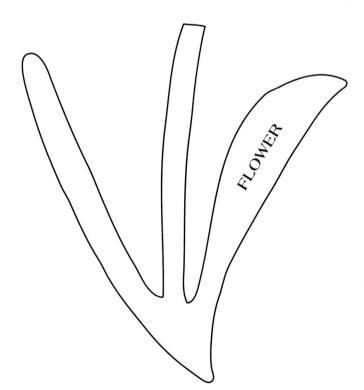

FLOWER

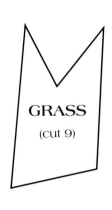

GRASS

(cut 9)

Diagram #1

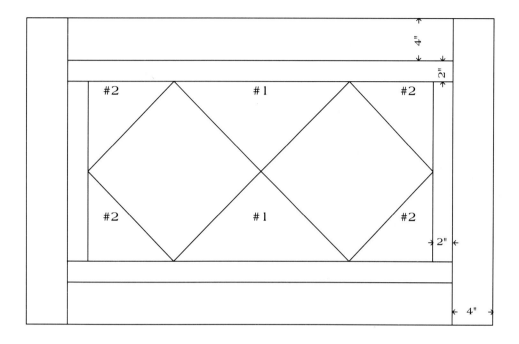

See Additional Patterns Section for these patterns:

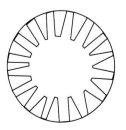

Page 152-3   Page 144-5   Page 154   Page 150-1

KELLY'S BUNNIES
52" x 57" finished size

FABRIC REQUIREMENTS
Bunnies
⅓ yd per bunny for body and
scraps for ears and tail
Background blocks
½ yd white and pastel plaid
½ yd pale blue
Blue floral borders and sashing
1⅓ yds (includes bias binding)
White and pastel floral borders
1 yd total of material

INSTRUCTIONS (Patterns: pages 80-82)
- Cut 2 – 15½" x 18" (+sa) white and pastel plaid blocks
- Cut 2 – 15½" x 18" (+sa) pale blue stripe blocks
- Cut 4 bunny bodies and arms – 2 regular and 2 reverse
- Cut 4 bunny ears and tails – 2 regular and 2 reverse
- Appliqué to blocks in following order:
  Tails, bodies, arms, and ears (I used a buttonhole stitch done with two strands of embroidery floss to appliqué to blocks).
- Cut 2 – 15½" x 1" (+sa) sashing strips
- Piecing sequence (with bunnies facing in – see *Diagram #1*)
- Blue block, sashing, plaid block
- Plaid, block, sashing, blue block
- Cut 3 – 37" x 1" (+sa) pieces of blue floral sashing
- Piecing sequence (with bunnies facing in – see *Diagram #1*)
- 37" x 1" sashing, bunnies, sashing, bunnies, sashing
- Cut 2 – 34" x 1" (+sa) pieces of blue floral sashing
- Sew to top and bottom
- Cut 2 – 34" x 1" (+sa) borders of white and pastel floral
- Cut 2 – 41" x 1" (+sa) borders of white and pastel floral
- Sew 34" x 1" borders to top and bottom
- Sew 41" x 1" borders to sides
- Cut 2 – 41" x 1" (+sa) borders of blue floral

- Cut 2 – 38" x 1" (+sa) borders of blue floral
- Sew 41" x 1" borders to sides
- Sew 38" x 1" borders to top and bottom
- Cut 2 – 38" x 6" (+sa) borders of white and pastel floral
- Cut 2 – 55" x 6" (+sa) borders of white and pastel floral
- Sew 38" x 6" borders to top and bottom
- Sew 55" x 6" borders to sides
- Cut 2 – 55" x 1" (+sa) borders of blue floral
- Cut 2 – 52" x 1" (+sa) borders of blue floral
- Sew 55" x 1" borders to sides
- Sew 52" x 1" borders to top and bottom
- Quilt and bind

Diagram #1

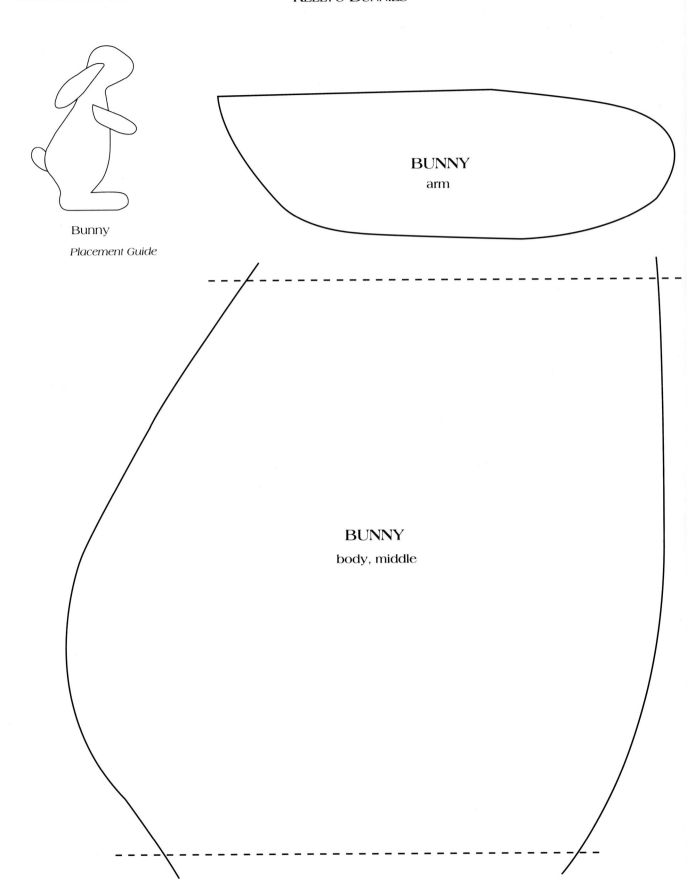

Bunny

Placement Guide

BUNNY
arm

BUNNY
body, middle

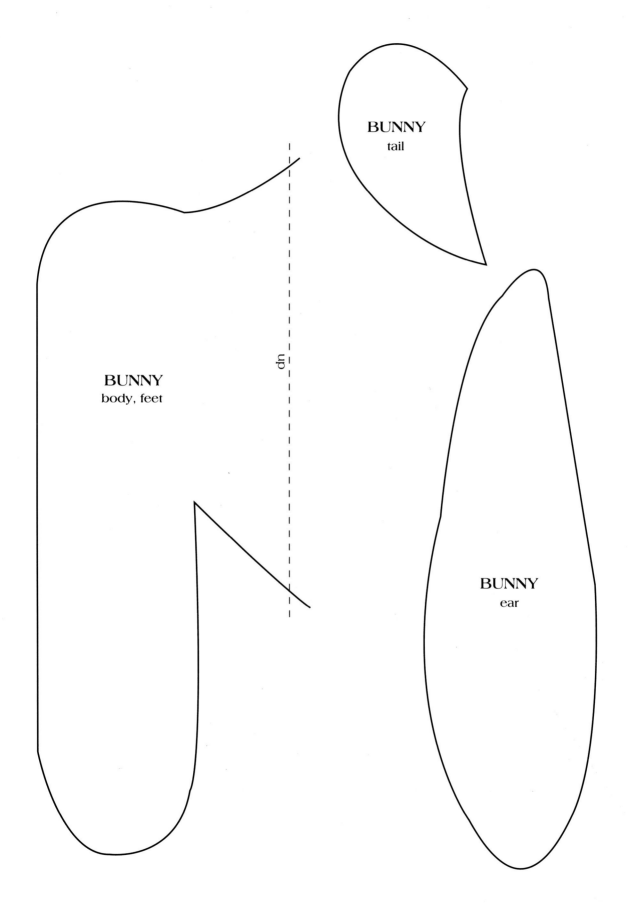

BUNNY
tail

BUNNY
body, feet

up

BUNNY
ear

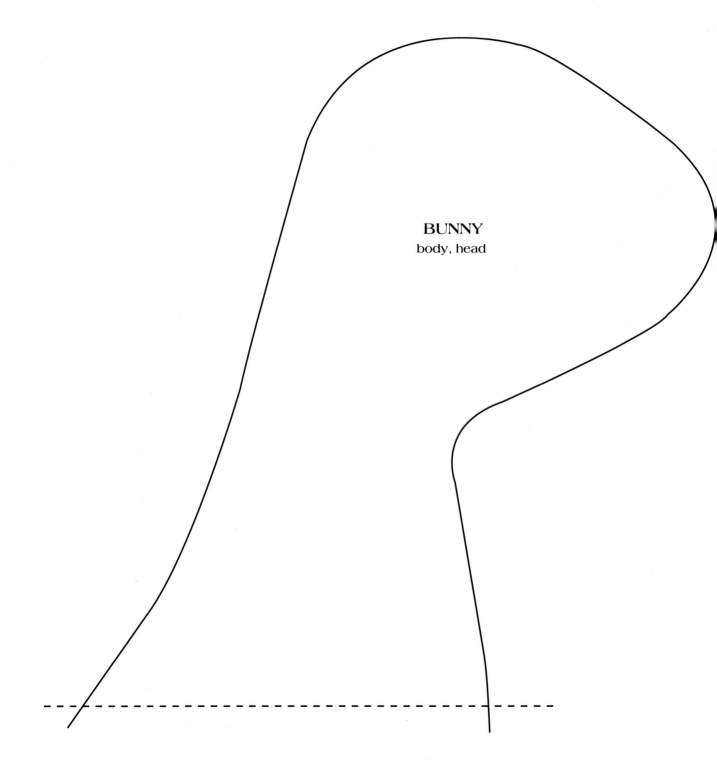

BUNNY
body, head

Full Quilt Diagram

LITTLE HOUSE
51" x 69" finished size

FABRIC REQUIREMENTS
¾ total or 6 – 12½" x 12½" pieces
of assorted blues
¾ yd for background squares and
triangles
⅜ yd for small border
1 yd for large border
¼ yd of 44" material for houses
Scraps for windows, doors & roofs
⅔ yd for bias binding
⅓ yd for straight binding

INSTRUCTIONS (Patterns: pages 152-153)
- Cut 4 – 12" (+sa) blue stripe squares
- Cut 2 – 12" (+sa) squares of 2 different blue prints
- Cut 2 – 12" (+sa) squares of off-white plaid
- Cut 6 triangles (Piece #1, pattern on page 140-141) of off-white plaid
- Cut 4 corner triangle (Piece #2, pattern on page 142) of off-white plaid
- Cut 3 houses and 3 reverse houses of off-white wide stripe
- Cut 3 roofs and 3 reverse roofs of lavender print
- Cut 6 windows and 6 reverse windows of gold print
- Cut 3 doors and 3 reverse doors of gold print
- Appliqué roofs, windows, and doors to houses
- Appliqué houses to blue stripe and blue print squares, set as diamonds
(See diagram or quilt)
- Using triangles and squares, piece together Rows 1-4 (Diagram 1);
both blue print squares are in Row 2
- Add bottom left and top right corner triangles (Piece #2)
(Top left and bottom right corners triangles are included in Rows 2 & 3)

- Cut 2 – 51" x 2" (+sa) borders of blue print
- Cut 2 – 38" x 2" (+sa) borders of blue print
- Sew 51" x 2" borders to sides
- Sew 38" x 2" borders to top and bottom
- Cut 2 – 38" x 7" (+sa) borders of off white plaid
- Cut 2 – 69" x 7" (+sa) borders of off white plaid
- Sew 38" x 7" borders to top and bottom
- Sew 69" x 7" borders to sides
- Quilt and bind

Diagram #1

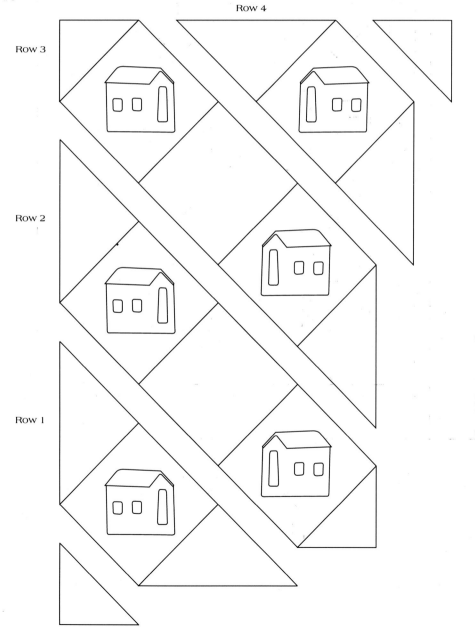

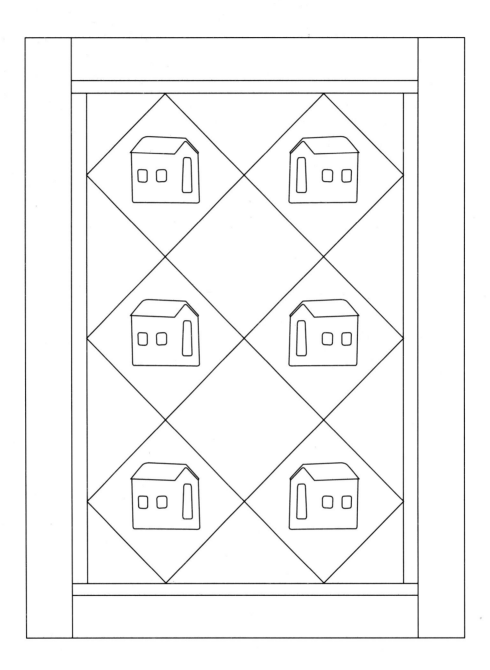

Page 152-3

LITTLE SILKIES WALLHANGING
21" x 24" finished size

FABRIC REQUIREMENTS
½ yd for background
⅛ yd for inner border
¼ yd for outer border
¼ yd for binding

INSTRUCTIONS (Patterns: pages 146-148)

- Cut a 18" x 15" (+sa) background
- Cut 1 rooster, 1 mama Silky, and 1 baby Silky
- Appliqué to background, referring to the photo
- Use buttonhole stitch around body of mama Silky
- Cut 2 – 15" x ½" (+sa) borders
- Cut 2 – 19" x ½" (+sa) borders
- Sew 15" x ½" borders to top and bottom
- Sew 19" x ½" borders to sides
- Cut 2 – 19" x 2½" (+sa) borders
- Cut 2 – 21" x 2½" (+sa) borders
- Sew 19" x 2½" borders to sides
- Sew 21" x 2½" borders to top and bottom

See Additional Patterns Section for these patterns:

Page 146   Page 147   Page 148

BASKETS & BERRIES
20" x 20" finished size

FABRIC REQUIREMENTS
⅛ yd for baskets
¼ yd total background
⅛ yd inner border
¼ yd outer border
⅛ yd binding (exactly)

INSTRUCTIONS (Patterns: pages 89, 155)
- Cut out 3 baskets, two with muslin background, one with plaid background
- Piece baskets in following manner
- Appliqué handle (piece 2) onto piece 1
  Sew 4 & 4R to 3
  Sew 6 & 6R to 5
  Join these units and add piece 7 to bottom
- Cut one 6½" (+sa) muslin square
- Appliqué 3 stalks with 3 berries each onto square
- Sew together
  Row 1 – basket with plaid background, basket with muslin background
  Row 2 – basket with muslin background, block with berries
- Join rows 1 & 2
- Cut 2 yellow borders ½" x 13" (+sa)
- Cut 2 yellow borders ½" x 14" (+sa)
- Sew ½" x 13" borders to top and bottom
- Sew ½" x 14" borders to sides
- Cut 2 plaid borders 3" x 14" (+sa)
- Cut 2 plaid borders 3" x 20" (+sa)
- Sew 3" x 14" borders to sides
- Sew 3" x 20" borders to top and bottom
- Quilt and bind

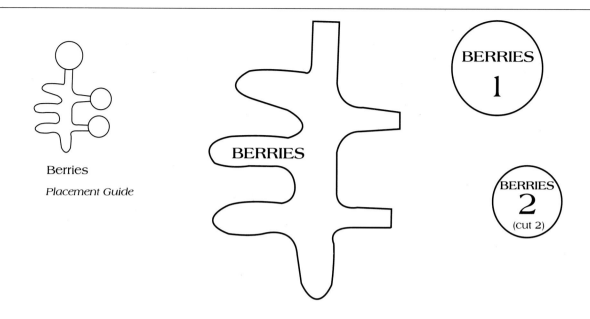

Berries

Placement Guide

BERRIES

BERRIES
1

BERRIES
2
(cut 2)

Full Quilt Diagram

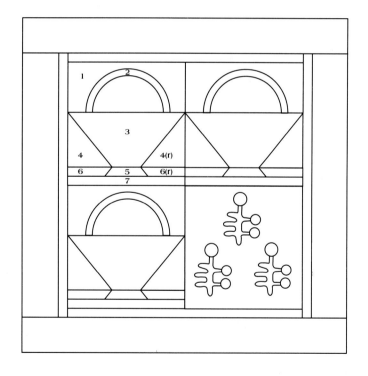

Page 155

SUMMERTIME (HOUSE AND TREE, ME AND THEE, II)
56" x 70" finished size

FABRIC REQUIREMENTS
  Center – 40" x 52" (+sa)
    2 yds total of lights, mediums, and darks – if stripped,
    1½ yds if solid piece is used
  Borders
    2½ yds of lights, mediums, and darks – if pieced,
    2 yds if solid piece is used
  House
    3 pieces – ¼ yd each
  Large tree
    ½ yd
  Sun
    3 pieces – ¼ yd each
  Vines
    ½ yd of 2 greens for bias vines
  Assorted scraps for remainder of appliquéd figures

INSTRUCTIONS (Patterns: pages 92-113, 143-145, 149, 156-157)

- Center – 40" x 52" (+sa)

  To get the uneven effect in the stripping, first make a paper pattern – a rectangle 40" x 52". Using the photo as a guide, draw lines roughly corresponding to the ones on the quilt. Number each segment (there should be 20 segments in all). To keep from getting confused, I would suggest cutting the segments from the paper pattern one at a time, then immediately cut the material pieces and sew them together. As your paper rectangle diminishes, the material rectangle will increase.

- Borders

  The borders on the two sides and top are 8" (+sa) wide, and the border on the bottom is 10" (+sa) wide. Once again I would suggest making a paper pattern first if you wish to piece the borders. The two sides are the same and the bottom and top are the same except for the width of the pieces. Sew the top and bottom to the center and then sew on the sides, mitering the corners.

- Center Rectangle Outline strips

  Using the same light material that you used for the center, piece a strip approximately 95" x 2". Press the edges under in an irregular manner, making your strip wider at some places and thinner at others. Appliqué in place using the photo as the guide.

- Appliqué

  Vines

  Cut ½" wide bias strips of each green and piece to make a 100" strip of each. Press under edges (your finished strips will each be ½" x 100") and appliqué in place on left and top borders according to photo. Appliqué flowers on vines.

  Sun

  Piece sun and appliqué onto quilt.

  House

  Piece house, appliqué on windows, doors and rose bush; then appliqué to background, having appliquéd large tree to background first.

  All other figures and objects

  Appliqué to background using the photo as a guide.

  Note: Remember to relax and have fun. Use my quilt and these patterns as just the guide for your personal summertime quilt!

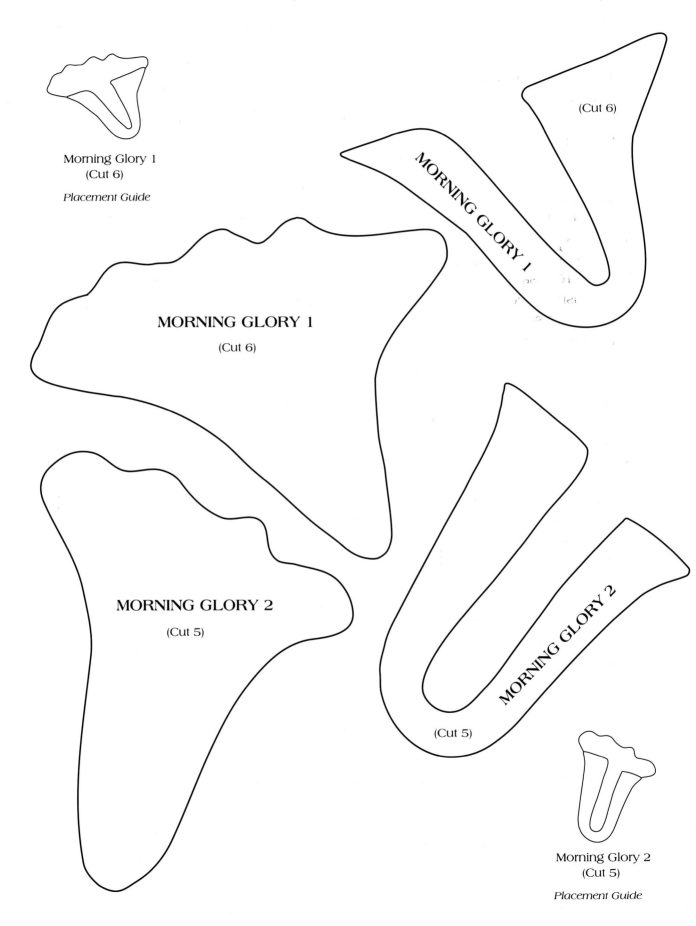

Morning Glory 1
(Cut 6)

Placement Guide

(Cut 6)

MORNING GLORY 1
(Cut 6)

MORNING GLORY 1

MORNING GLORY 2
(Cut 5)

MORNING GLORY 2

(Cut 5)

Morning Glory 2
(Cut 5)

Placement Guide

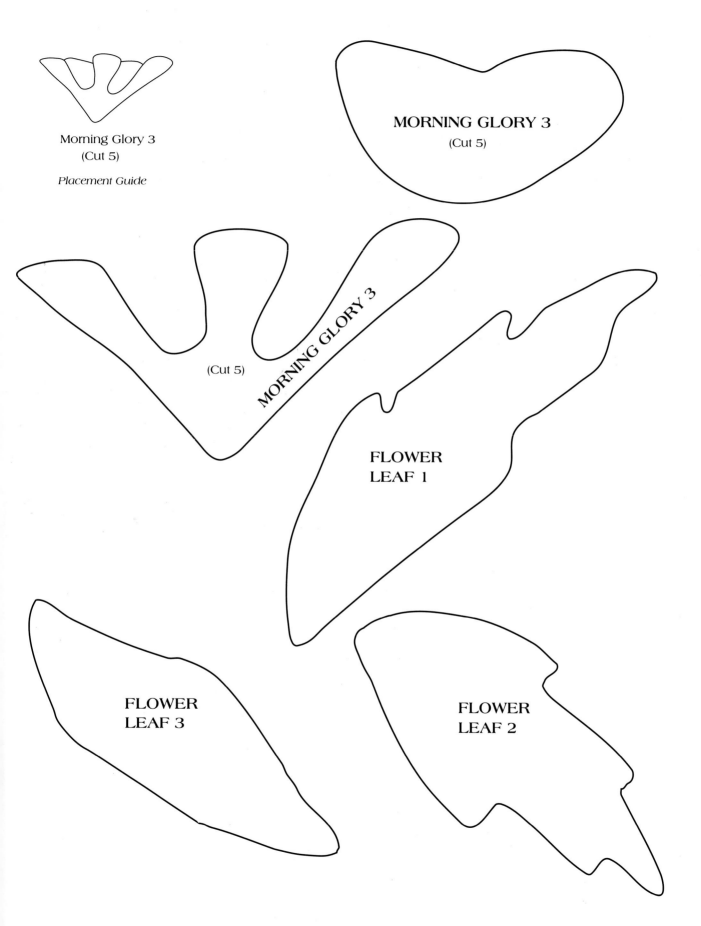

Morning Glory 3
(Cut 5)

Placement Guide

MORNING GLORY 3
(Cut 5)

(Cut 5)

MORNING GLORY 3

FLOWER
LEAF 1

FLOWER
LEAF 3

FLOWER
LEAF 2

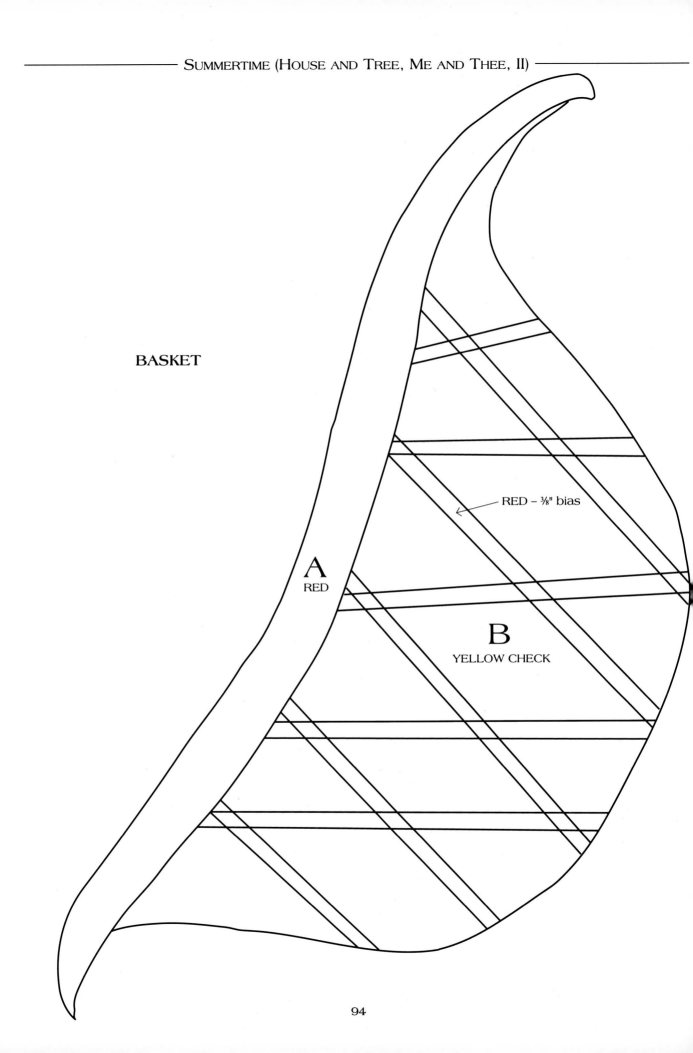

BASKET

RED – ⅜" bias

A
RED

B
YELLOW CHECK

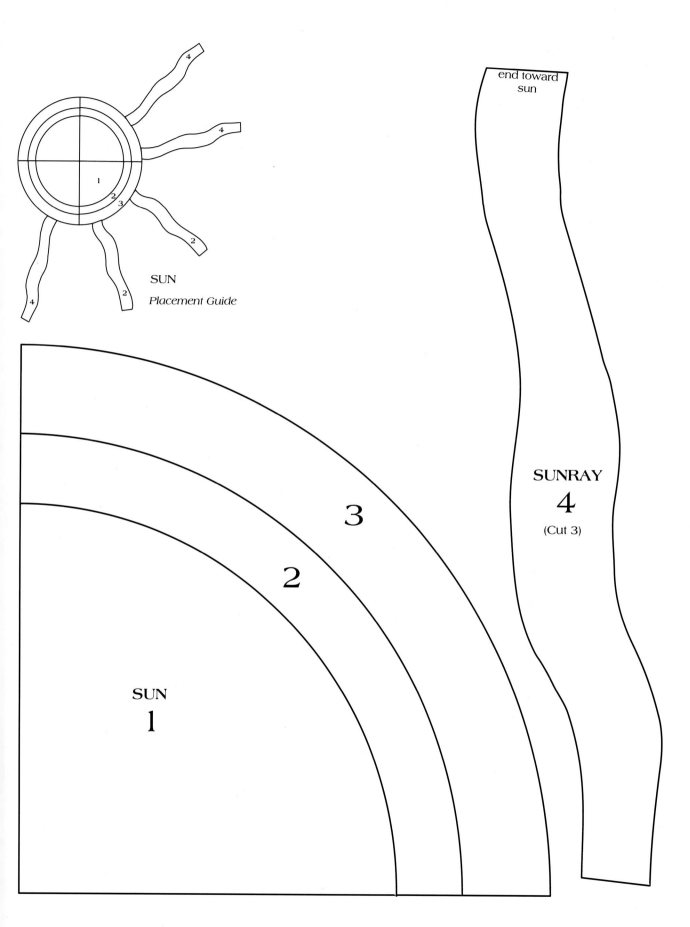

SUN

Placement Guide

end toward
sun

SUNRAY

4

(Cut 3)

SUN

1

2

3

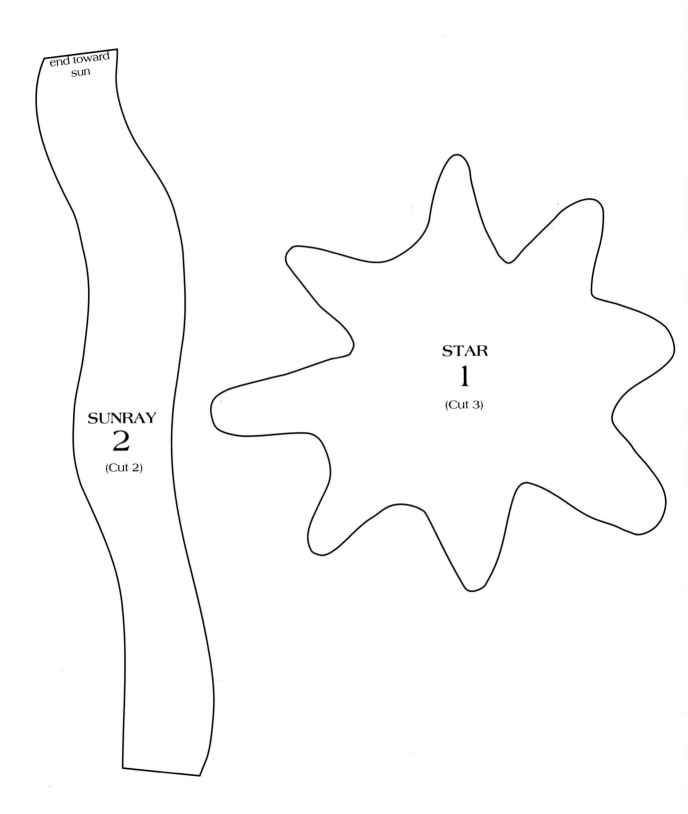

end toward sun

SUNRAY
2
(Cut 2)

STAR
1
(Cut 3)

*Cut about 25 leaves;
make about half reverse leaves*

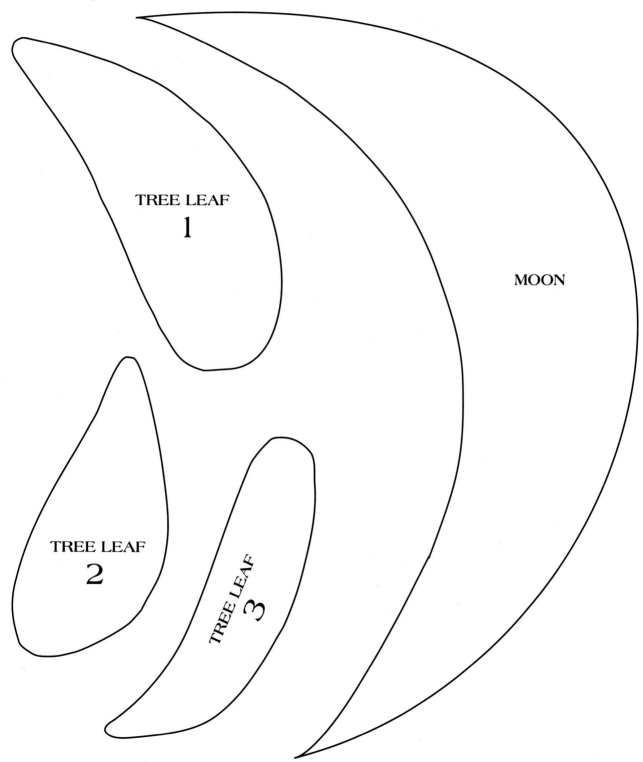

TREE LEAF
1

MOON

TREE LEAF
2

TREE LEAF
3

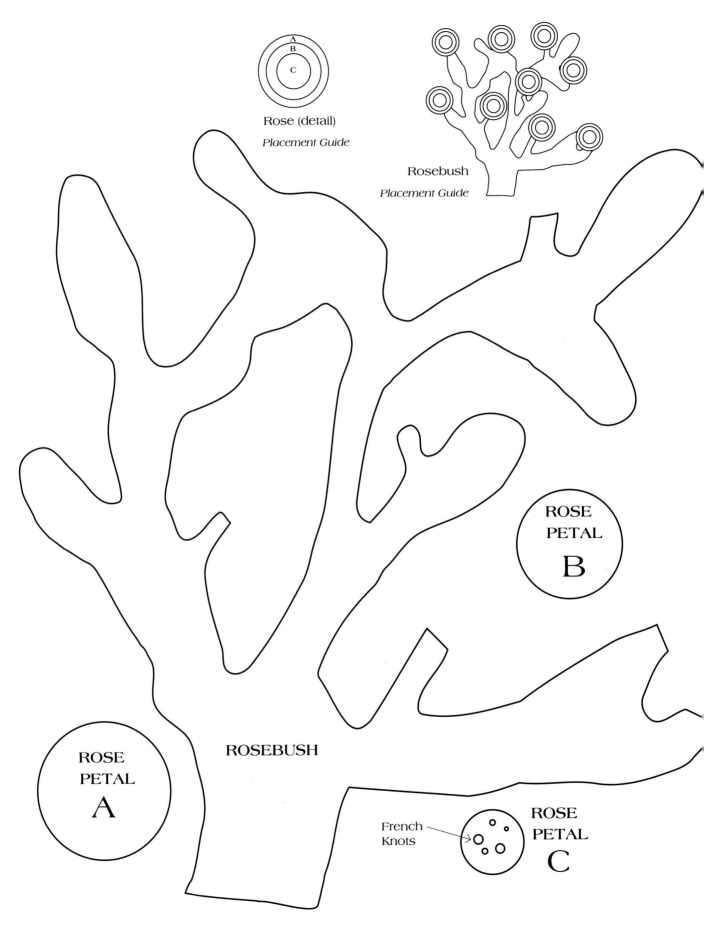

Rose (detail)

Placement Guide

Rosebush

Placement Guide

ROSE
PETAL
B

ROSE
PETAL
A

ROSEBUSH

French
Knots

ROSE
PETAL
C

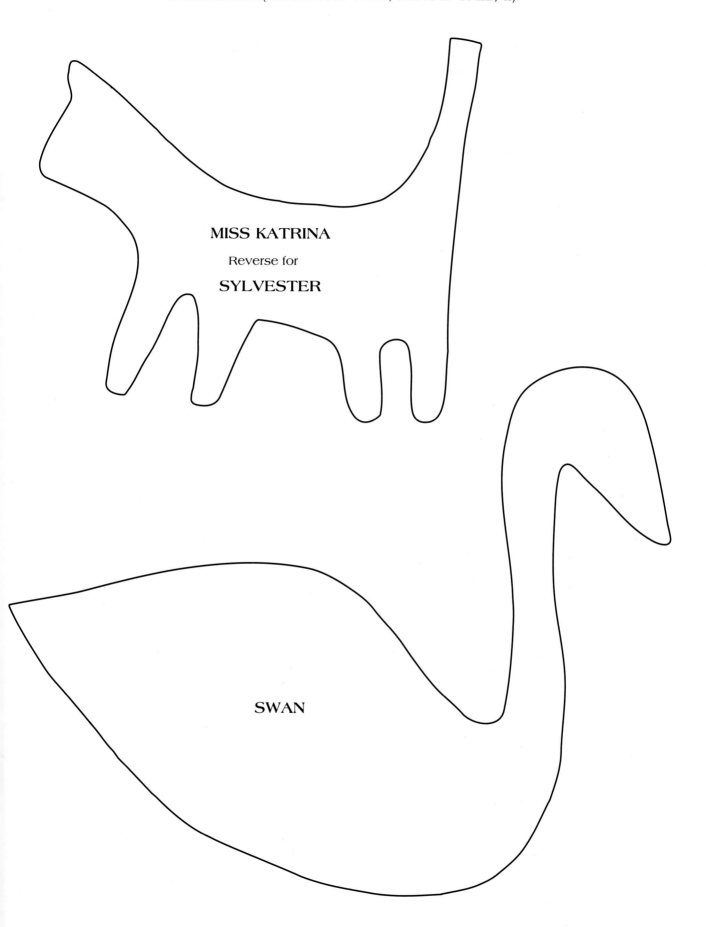

MISS KATRINA

Reverse for

SYLVESTER

SWAN

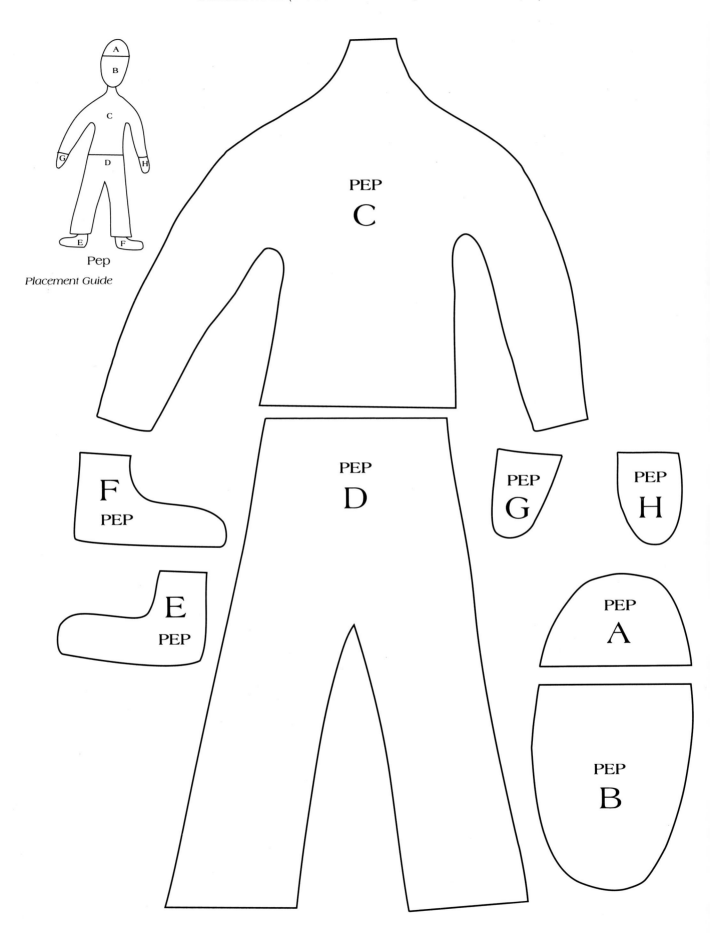

Pep

Placement Guide

PEP C

PEP D

PEP F

PEP E

PEP G

PEP H

PEP A

PEP B

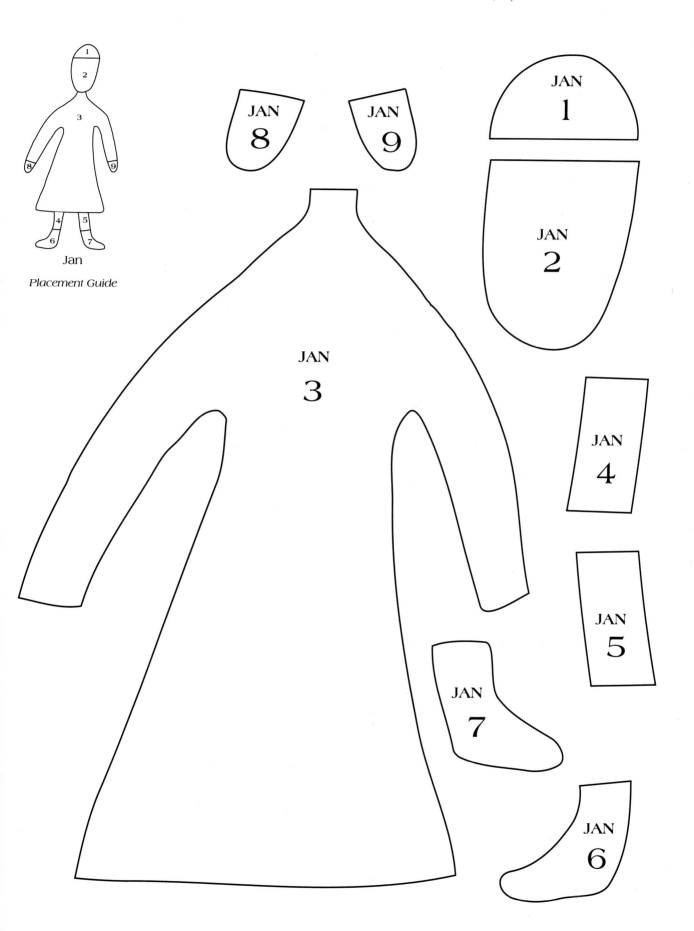

Jan

Placement Guide

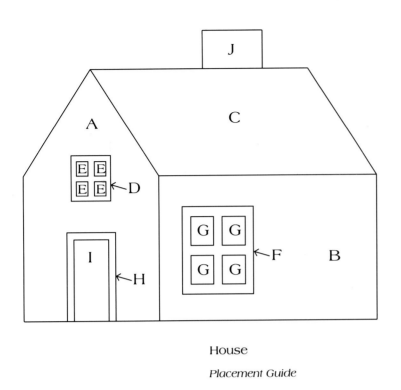

House

Placement Guide

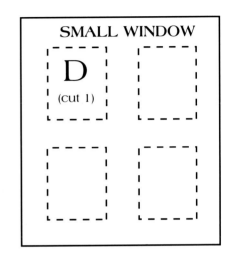

SMALL WINDOW

D
(cut 1)

E
(cut 4)

G
(cut 4)

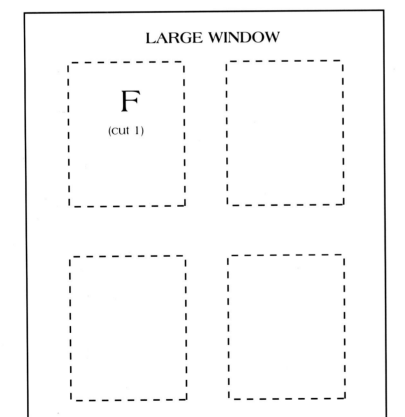

LARGE WINDOW

F
(cut 1)

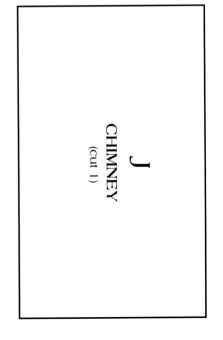

J
CHIMNEY
(cut 1)

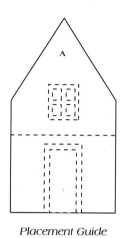

Placement Guide

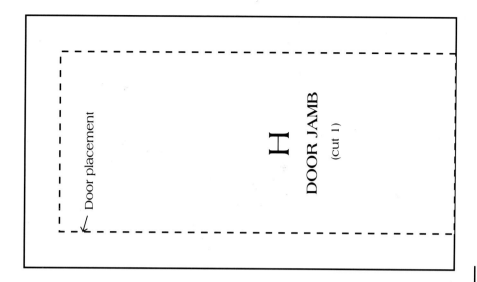

H
DOOR JAMB
(cut 1)

Door placement

Door Jamb
Placement

A (BOTTOM)
HOUSE FRONT
(cut 1)

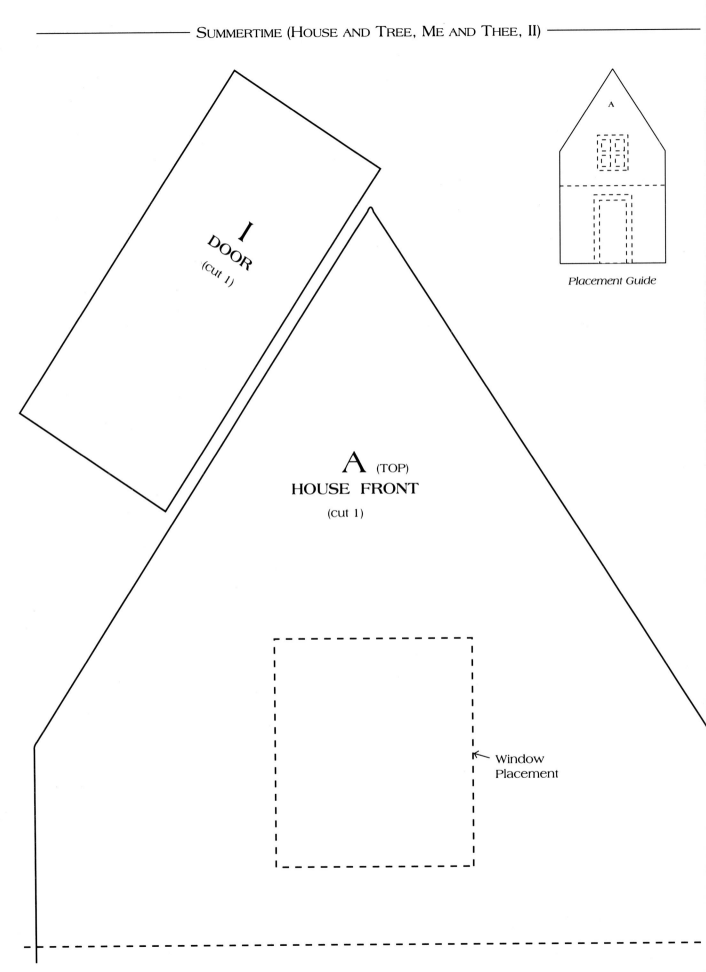

I
DOOR
(cut 1)

A (TOP)
HOUSE FRONT
(cut 1)

Window
Placement

Placement Guide

A

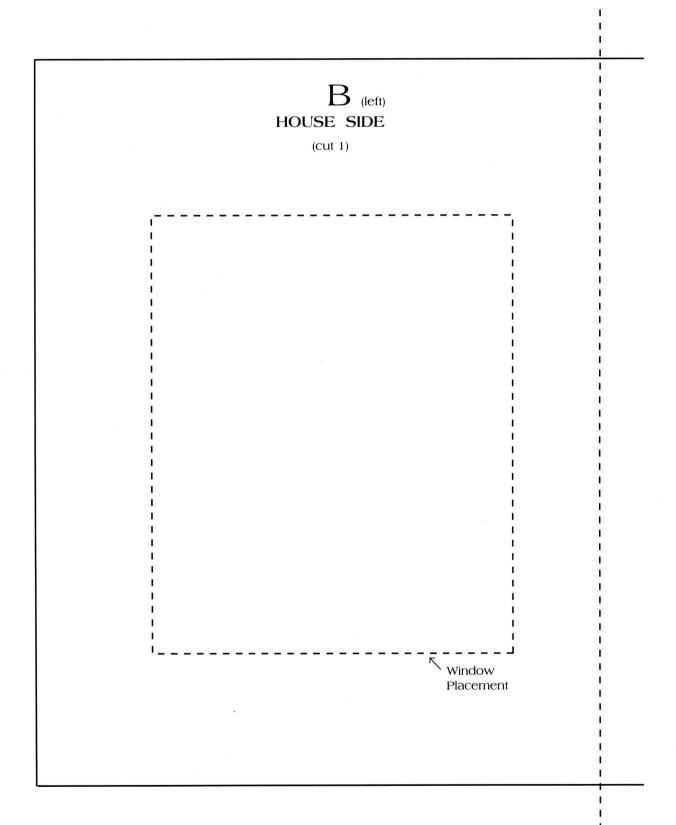

B (left)
HOUSE SIDE
(cut 1)

Window
Placement

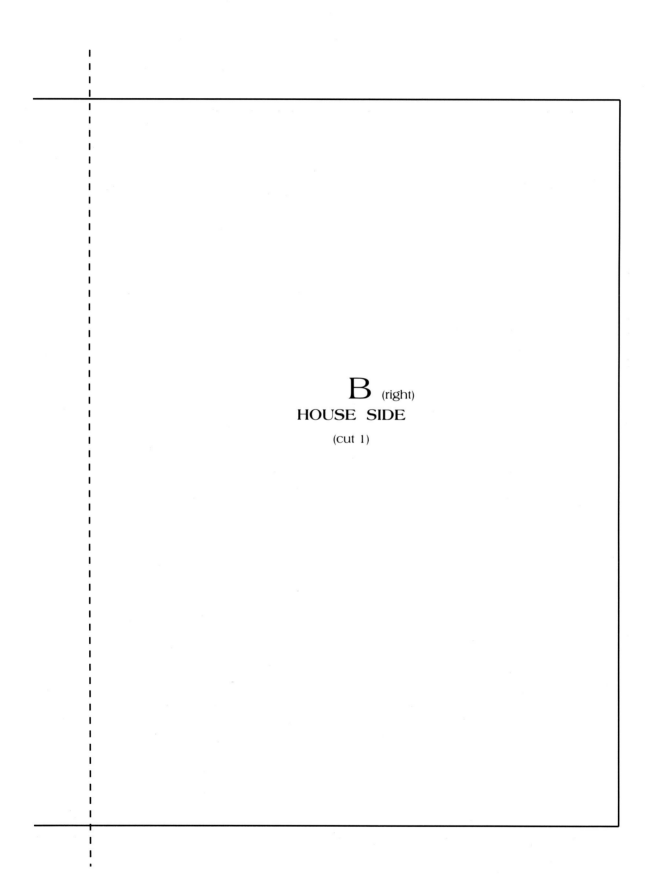

B (right)
HOUSE SIDE
(cut 1)

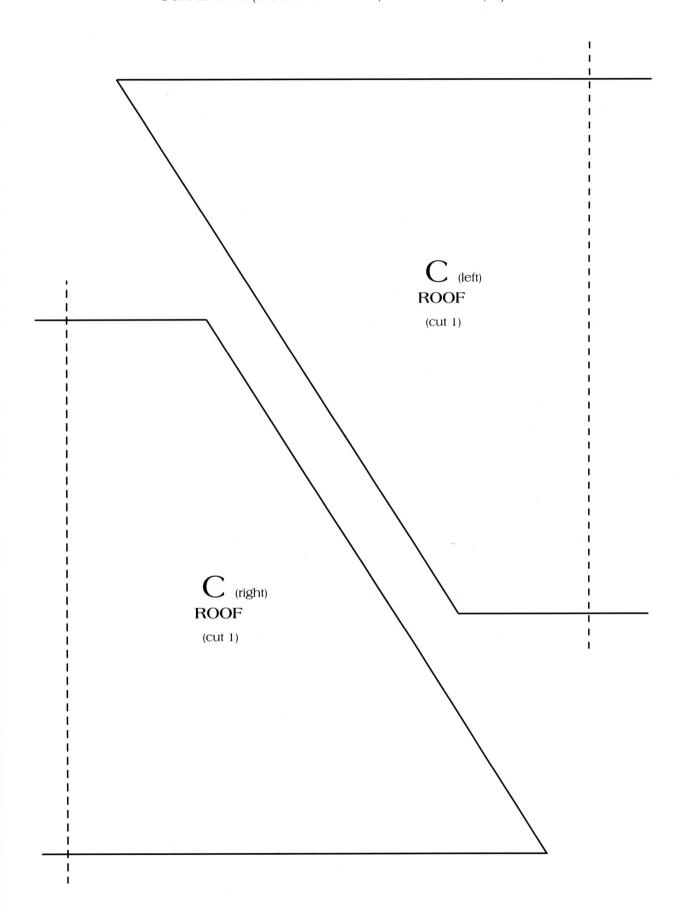

C (left)
ROOF
(cut 1)

C (right)
ROOF
(cut 1)

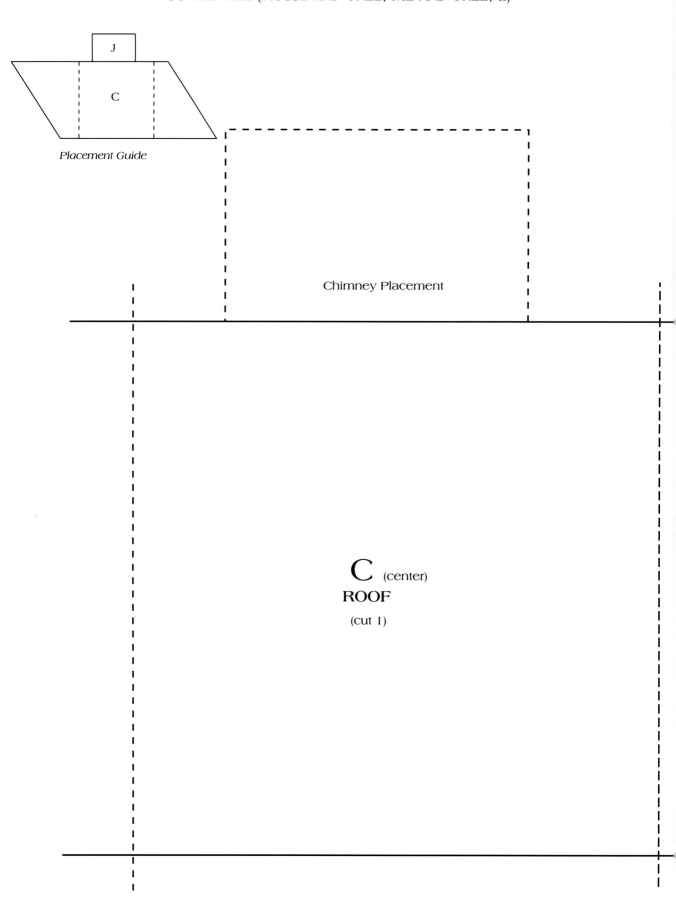

J

C

Placement Guide

Chimney Placement

C (center)

ROOF

(cut 1)

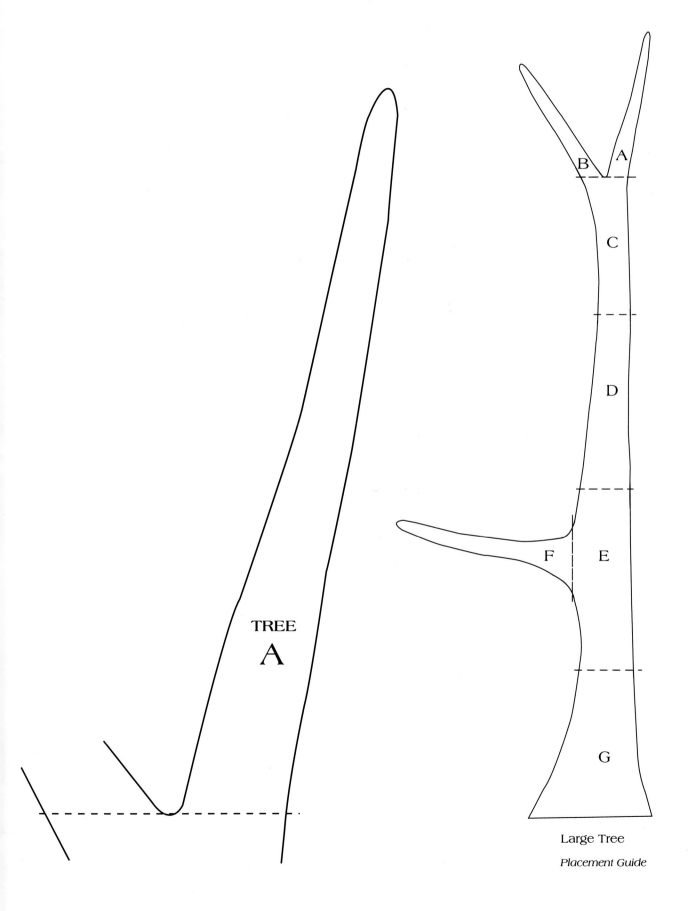

TREE

A

B A

C

D

F E

G

Large Tree

Placement Guide

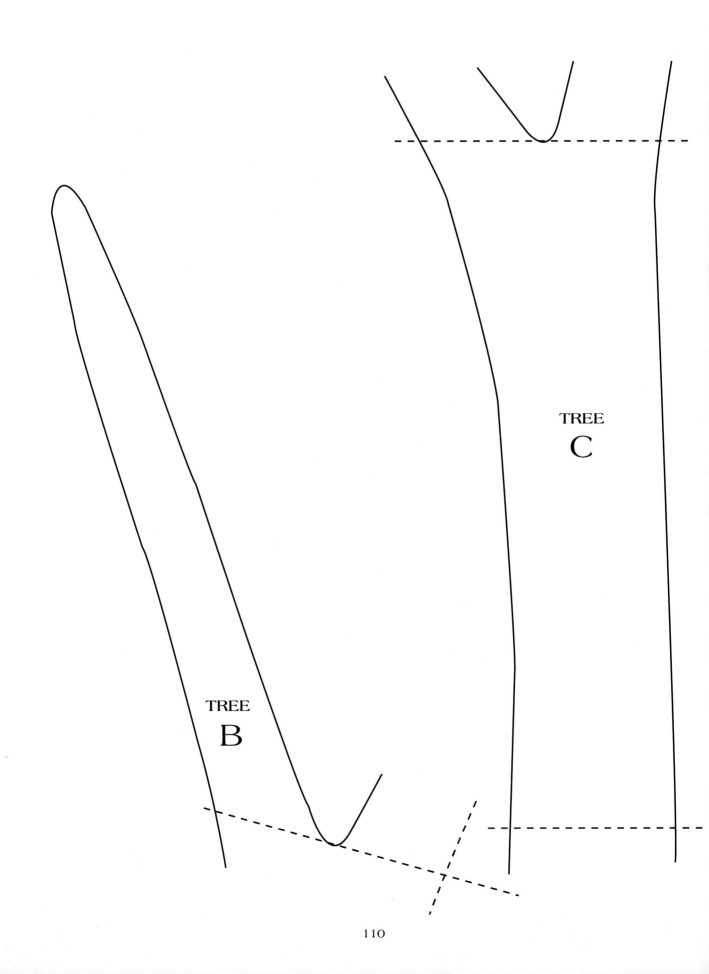

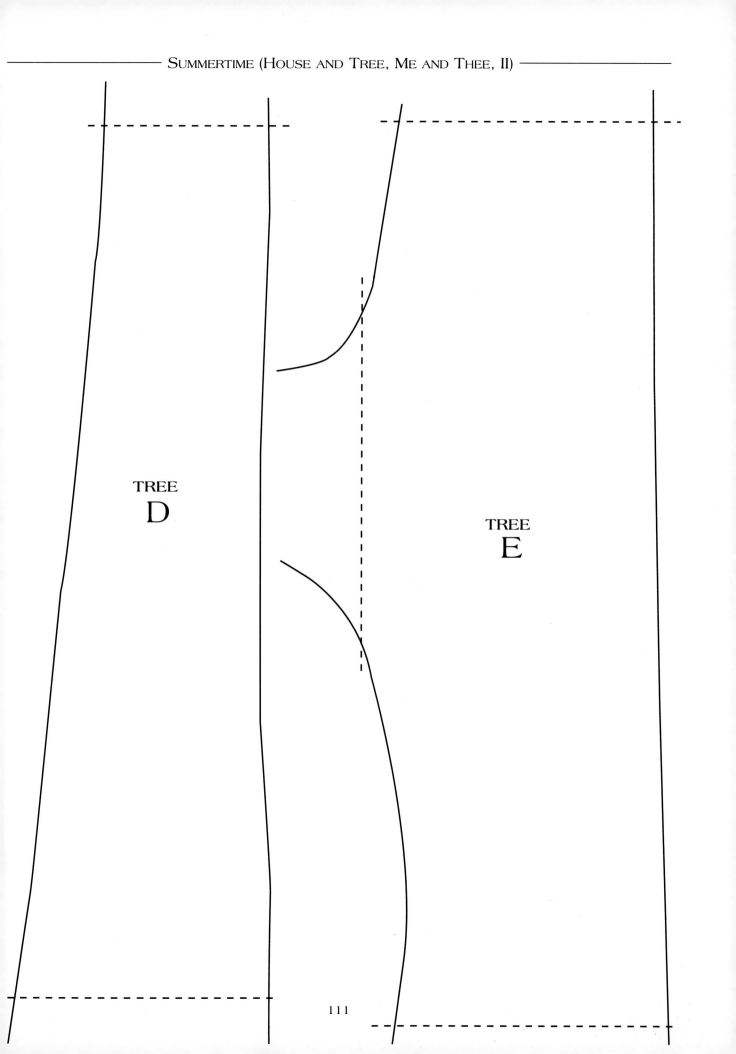

TREE
D

TREE
E

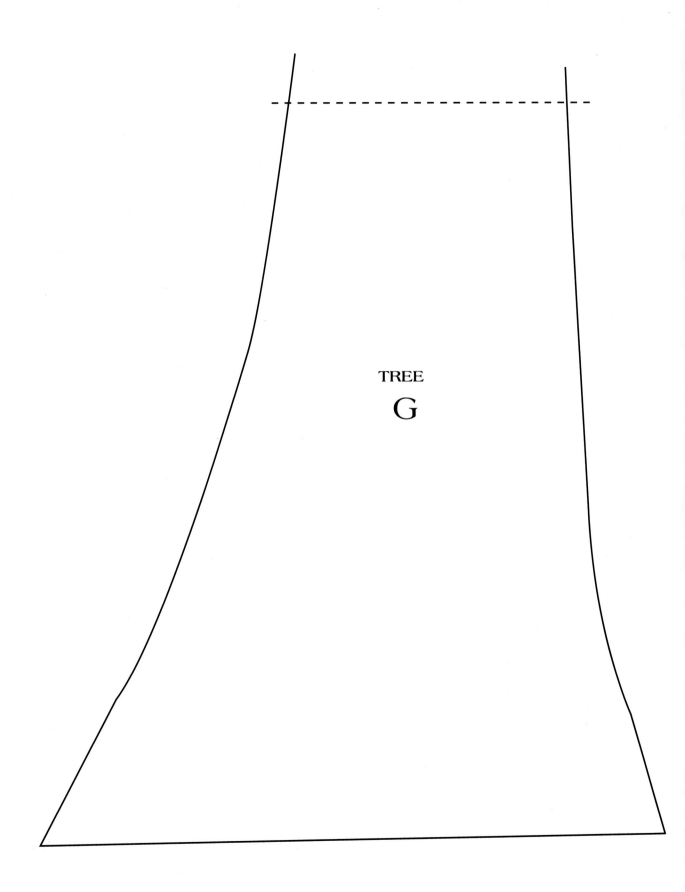

TREE
G

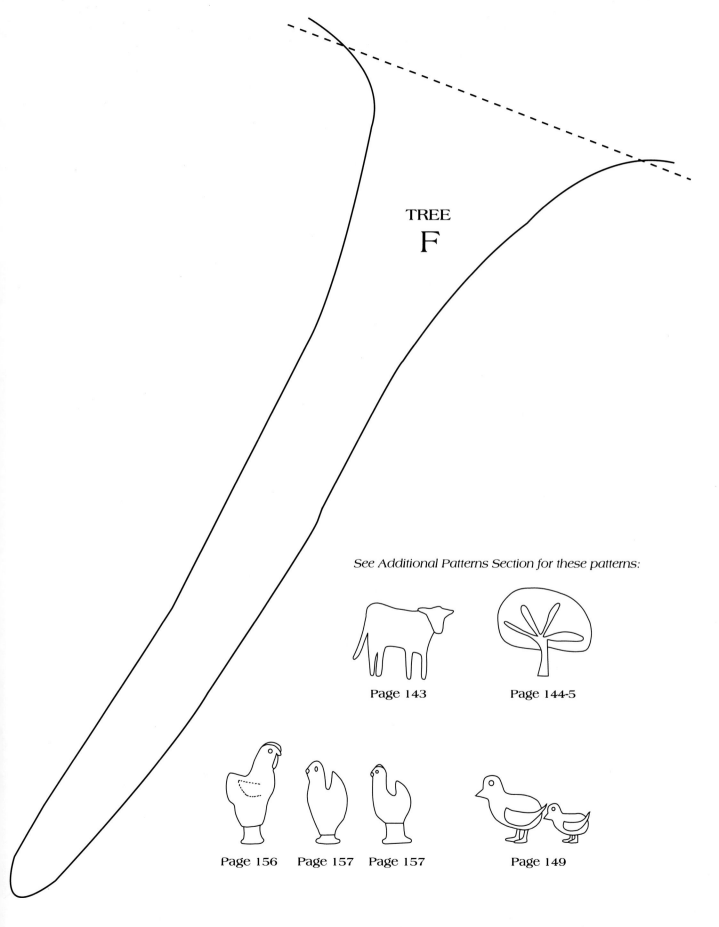

TREE
F

See Additional Patterns Section for these patterns:

Page 143   Page 144-5

Page 156   Page 157   Page 157   Page 149

BRIAN'S DUCK SAMPLER
10" x 9" finished size

FABRIC REQUIREMENTS
   Scrap of muslin for block
   Blue, red, and yellow floss

INSTRUCTIONS (Pattern: page 115)
- Cut 10" x 9" (+sa) muslin block
- Tan dye or stain if you wish. A paste of dye and water dropped straight onto material will make nice stains.
- Using stem stitch, embroider body in blue, bill and feet in yellow, and letters and numbers in red. Add name and date and finish off.

BRIAN'S DUCK

LOG CABIN
70" x 90" finished size

FABRIC REQUIREMENTS
  Log Cabin blocks
  ½ yd of lights and
  ½ yd of darks per block
  (This will include enough left
  over to piece the large border
  and the binding). You will probably have quite a few scraps,
  but I wanted to make sure you
  had enough material.
  Small border
  ⅓ yd
  Large border
  1 yd (if you want it all one color)
  Centers of Log blocks
  ⅓ yd – Blue
  ¼ yd – Pink
  ¼ yd – Yellow
  Binding
  ½ yd (if you want it all one color)

INSTRUCTIONS (Patterns: pages 118-121, 143-145, 149-151, 154-157)
  • Cut 4 yellow rectangles: two 5" x 8" (+sa), one 8" x 9" (+sa),
    one 8" x 8" (+sa).
  • Cut 2 hearts (page 18), the smaller (A) green, the larger (B) blue
  • Appliqué the green heart onto the blue, then appliqué them onto
    a 5" x 8" yellow rectangle
  • Cut out the flower (page 19) – green stem, pink and blue blossom,
  • Appliqué onto 8" x 9" yellow rectangle
  • Cut out blue duck (page 149, duck #1) with yellow wing and feet
  • Appliqué onto 8" x 8" yellow square
  • Cut out green Baby Silky (page 157, #3), yellow beak and "feet," and red comb
  • Appliqué to 5" x 8" yellow rectangle
  • Cut 4 pink rectangles the following sizes: 8" x 9" (+sa), 6" x 8" (+sa), 5" x 8" (+sa),
    9" x 8" (+sa)

- Cut out blue rooster (page 156), yellow beak and "feet," red comb
- Appliqué to 6" x 8" pink rectangle
- Cut out green Mama Silky (page 157) and yellow beak and "feet"
- Appliqué to 5" x 8" pink rectangle with buttonhole stitch using 1 strand of charcoal embroidery floss
- Cut out green cow (page 143) with cream colored spots
- Appliqué spots and head to body
- Appliqué cow to 9" x 8" pink rectangle
- Cut out yellow tree with blue cherries (page 154)
- Appliqué tree and cherries to 8" x 9" pink rectangle
- Cut out 3 blue squares the following sizes: 8" x 8" (+sa), 8" x 8" (+sa), 9" x 9" (+sa)
- Cut out pink circle and yellow sun (page 150-151)
- Appliqué sun to circle
- Appliqué circle to 8" x 8" blue square
- Cut out pink tree "leaves" and white trunk (page 144-145)
- Appliqué trunk to "leaves"
- Appliqué total tree to 8" x 8" blue square
- Cut out pink plaid house, dark blue roof, yellow chimney, medium blue door, and white plaid windows
- Appliqué roof, chimney, doors, and windows to house (page 120)
- Appliqué total house to 9" x 9" blue square
- Cut out basket block using blue background and pink basket (page 155)
  Piecing sequence:
    Appliqué handle (2) to piece #1
    4, 3, 4r
    6, 5, 6r
    Sew the above units together and add 7
- Log Cabin block
  All logs are cut 2" wide. This does include seam allowance. Finished logs will be 1½" wide.
- Make a 20" (+sa) square template.
- Using *Diagram #1* and photo as a reference for lights and darks, sew logs to rectangles and squares so that each block is at least 20" (+sa) square. As the rectangles and squares are not a uniform size, it will often be necessary to add an uneven number of logs. Lay 20" (+sa) square template on each block and trim to size of template.
- Cut kitten (page 121) and appliqué onto basket block, referring to photo.
- Sew Log Cabin blocks together in order seen in photo and *Diagram #1*.
- Cut 2 – 80" x 1" (+sa) pink plaid borders
- Cut 2 – 62" x 1" (+sa) pink plaid borders
- Sew 80" x 1" borders to sides

- Sew 62" x 1" borders to top and bottom
- Cut 2 – 62" x 4" (+sa) borders varying darks and lights
- Cut 2 – 90" x 4" (+sa) borders varying darks and lights
- Sew 62" x 4" borders to top and bottom
- Sew 90" x 4" borders to sides
- Quilt and bind

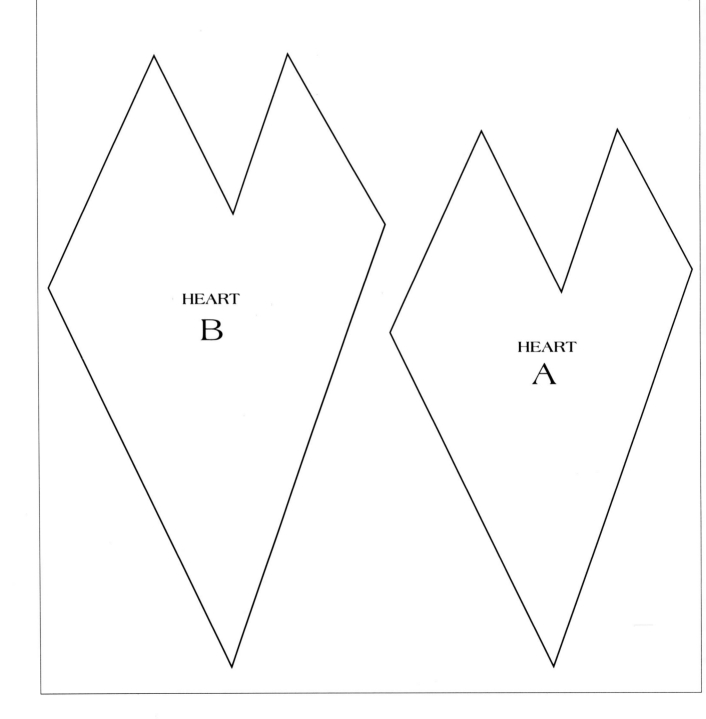

HEART
B

HEART
A

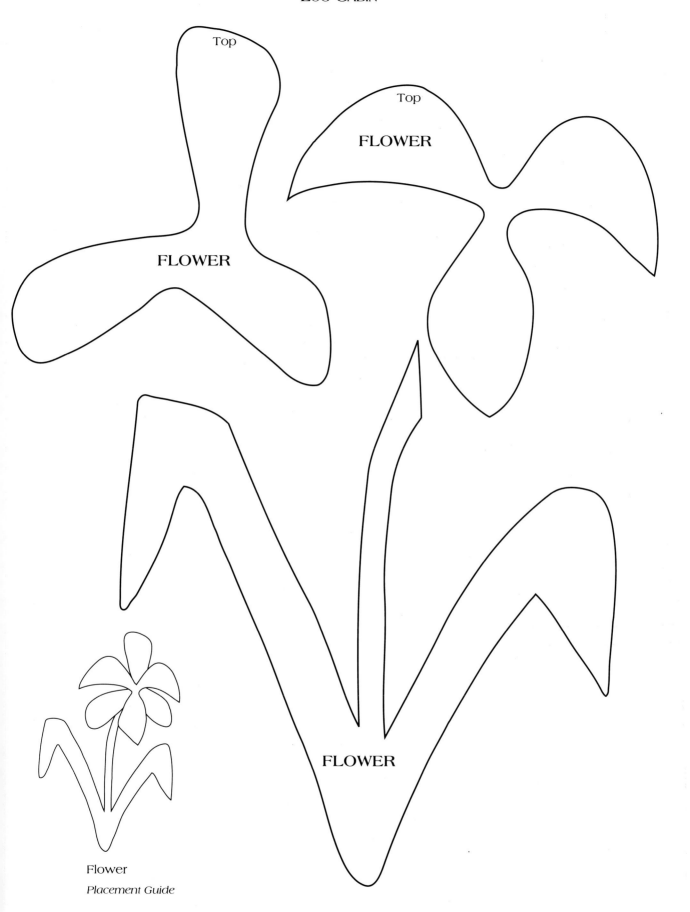

Top

Top

FLOWER

FLOWER

FLOWER

FLOWER

Flower

Placement Guide

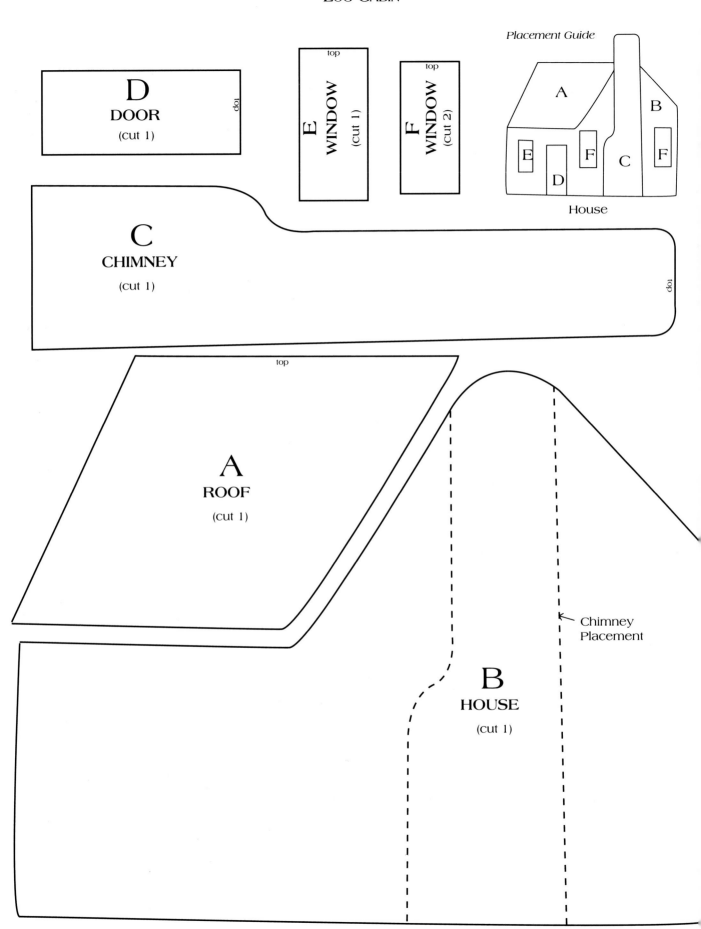

D
DOOR
(cut 1)

E
WINDOW
(cut 1)
top

F
WINDOW
(cut 2)
top

Placement Guide

A

B

E
F
D
C
F

House

C
CHIMNEY
(cut 1)

top

A
ROOF
(cut 1)

top

B
HOUSE
(cut 1)

Chimney
Placement

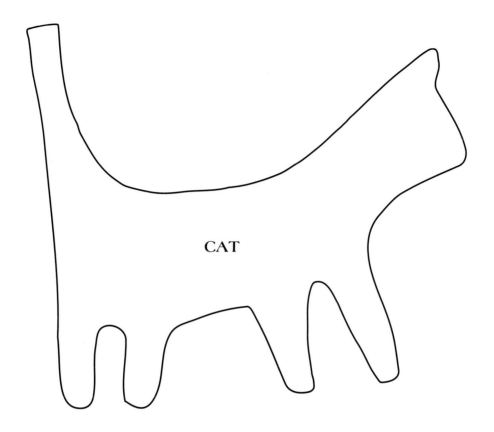

CAT

See Additional Patterns Section for these patterns:

Page 149

Page 157   Page 156   Page 157

Page 143

Page 154

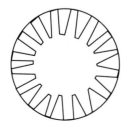

Page 150-1

Page 144-5

Page 155

Diagram #1: Full Quilt

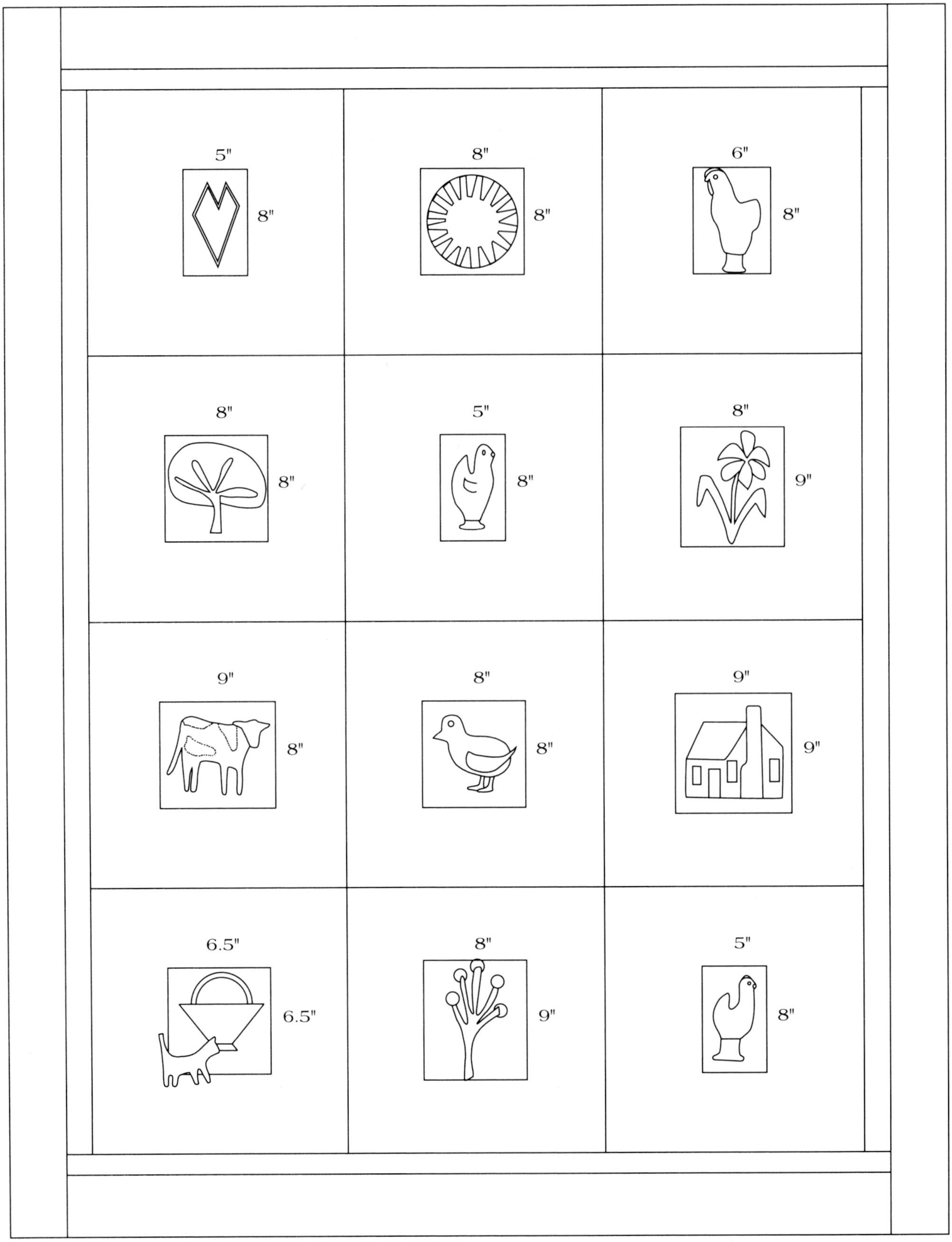

YOUNG MAN'S FANCY

88" x 95½" finished size

FABRIC REQUIREMENTS

Heart blocks

I have pieced six different color combinations and repeated each color combination (i.e. – yellow and blue block, peach and green block, etc.) eight times. I am giving you the fabric requirements for eight heart blocks of each color combination. You will need to repeat this six times.

Outside triangle

½ yd

Background triangle around heart

¼ yd

Heart

¼ yd

Triangles around edge of quilt

1 yd

Lattice strips, small border & 1 block

2 yds

Outside border if tied

2 yds

Outside border if quilted

1⅓ yd

INSTRUCTIONS (Patterns: pages 126, 128)

- Cut out and piece 48 heart blocks

   (I have chosen to make six repeat blocks in eight different color combinations but 48 different blocks would be great if you have an assortment of pastel fabrics.)

- Piece 48 blocks piecing sequence:

   E, D, F

   Fr, Dr, Er

   Sew these 2 units together

   B, C, Br

   Sew this unit to the first one.

   Add piece A on 4 sides to complete block

- Cut 22 triangles (Piece #1, page 128) of white and pastel print
- Cut 1 – 9" (+sa) square of white and pastel plaid
- Cut 54 – 9" x 1¼" (+sa) lattice strips of same plaid
- Sew triangles, blocks, and 9" x 1¼" lattice strips into diagonal rows as seen in *Diagram #1* (page 127). The 9" plaid square is the third block in Row #7
- Cut 4 Piece #2 (page 128) of white and pastel plaid for Corner Sets
- Make 4 Corner Sets consisting of Piece #1 joined by 1 Piece #2 (see *Diagram #1*)
- Cut approximately 580" of 1¼" (+sa) lattice stripping of white and pastel plaid
- Sew together Rows 1-9 with lattice strips and add Corner Sets as seen in *Diagram #2* and *Diagram #3* (page 129)
- Cut 2 – 74½" x ¾" (+sa) borders of white and pastel plaid
- Cut 2 – 90½" x ¾" (+sa) borders of white and pastel plaid
- Sew 74 – 12" x ¾" borders to top and bottom
- Sew 90½" x ¾" borders to sides
- Cut 2 – 90½" x 6" (+sa) borders of white and pastel print*
- Cut 2 – 88" x 2½" (+sa) borders of white and pastel print*
- Sew 90½" x 6" borders to sides
- Sew 88" x 2½" borders to top and bottom

*Brenda wanted her quilt to be a comfort, so I used a 3½ lb. wool batt covered with cheesecloth. Because a binding is very difficult to sew to this, I added 3" to the outside borders so I would have plenty of fabric to turn it under on the back. If you do this, you'll need to make your borders 90½" x 9" (+sa) and 94" x 5½" (+sa).

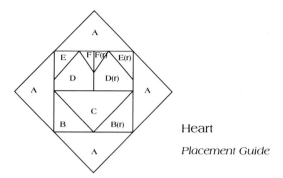

Heart

Placement Guide

Full Quilt Diagram

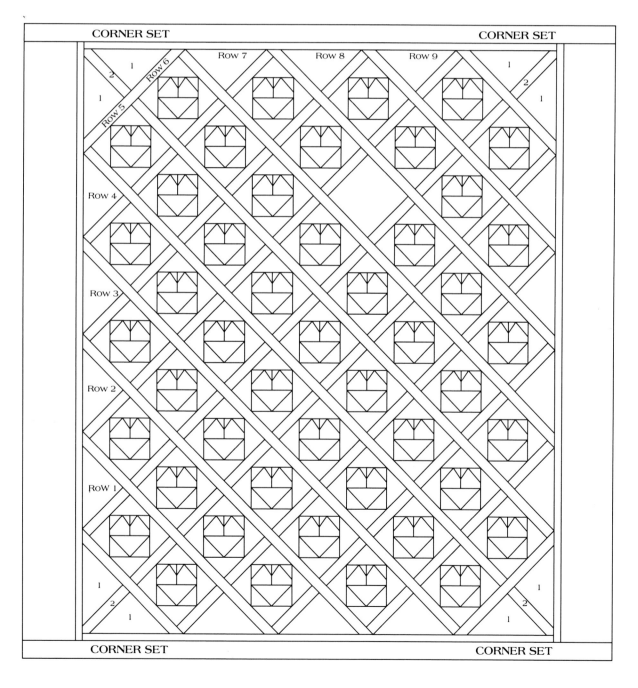

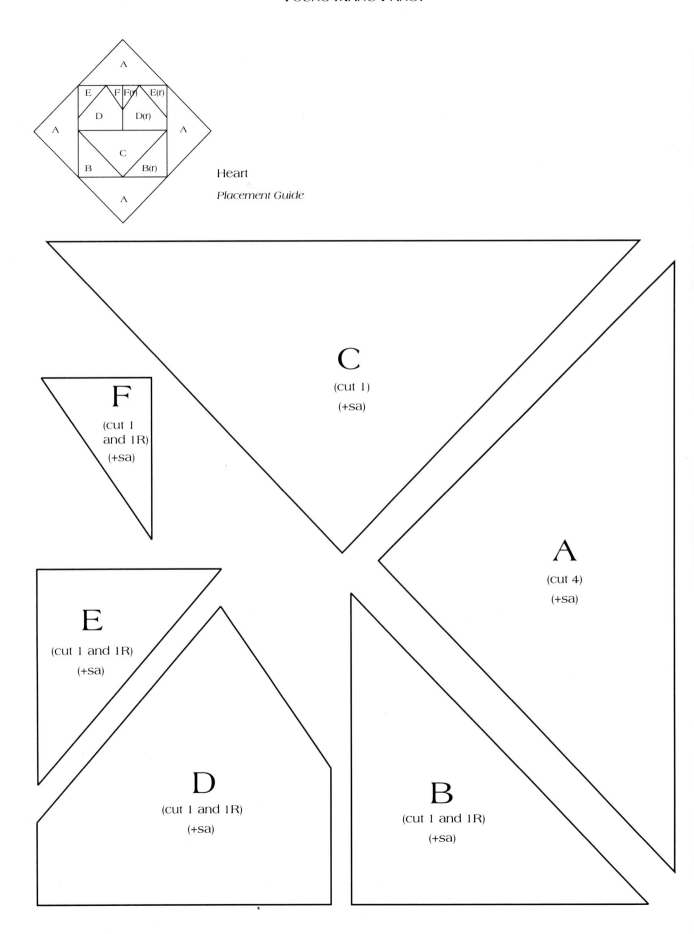

Heart
Placement Guide

A
(cut 4)
(+sa)

C
(cut 1)
(+sa)

F
(cut 1
and 1R)
(+sa)

E
(cut 1 and 1R)
(+sa)

D
(cut 1 and 1R)
(+sa)

B
(cut 1 and 1R)
(+sa)

Diagram #1

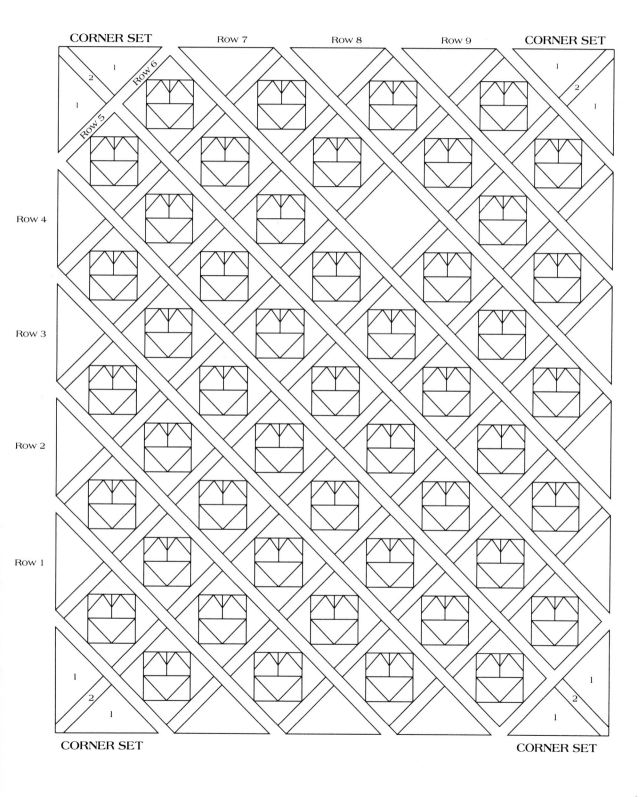

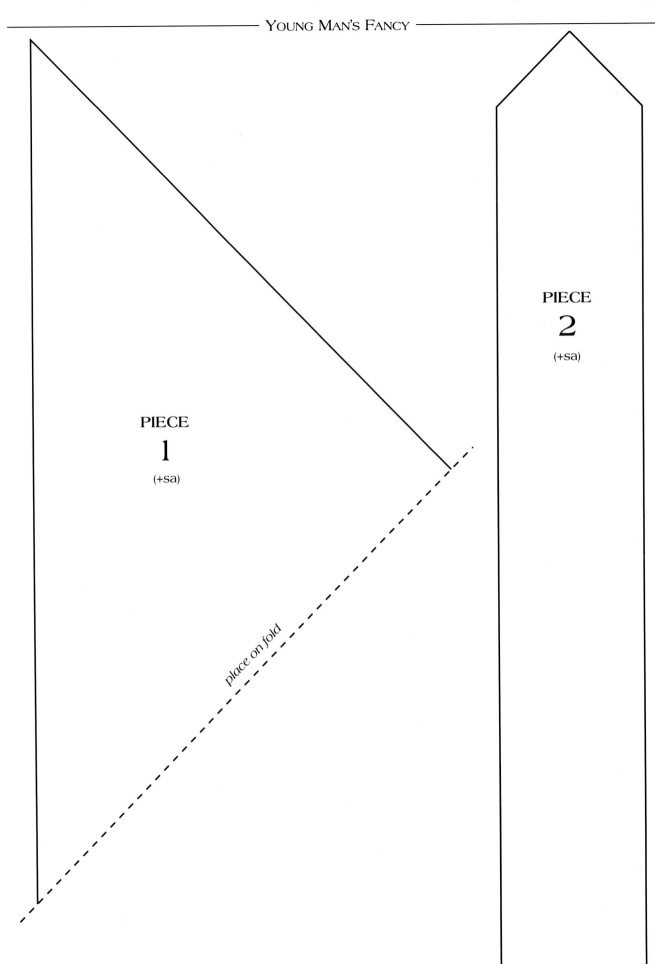

PIECE

1

(+sa)

PIECE

2

(+sa)

place on fold

Diagram #2

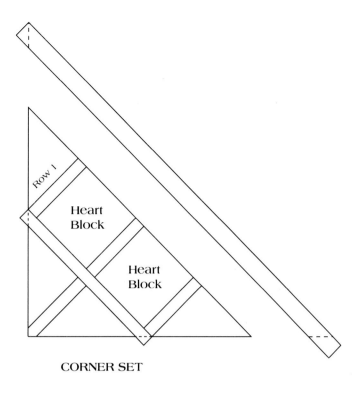

CORNER SET

Diagram #3

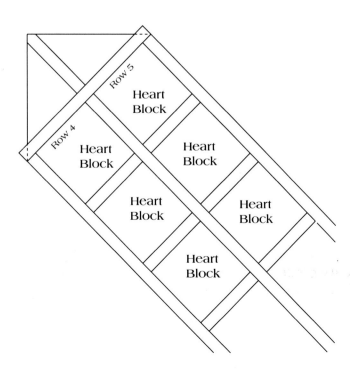

YOUNG MAN'S FANCY (SMALL)
28" x 34" finished size

FABRIC REQUIREMENTS
⅛ yd for hearts and background
   or assorted scraps
⅓ yd total fabric for large triangles
   around hearts
⅓ yd total assorted fabric for
   triangles around border
⅛ yd inner border
⅓ yd outer border
¼ yd binding

INSTRUCTIONS (Patterns: pages 132-133)
- Cut out and piece 4 heart blocks from Young Man's Fancy using same piecing, sequence discussed on page 124 (See *Diagram #1*, page 131), but omitting one piece A from each block (See *Diagram #2*, page 131)
- Using *Diagram #2*, piece 2 rectangles consisting of two heart blocks each
- Join rectangles
- Cut 2 – 19" x 1" (+sa) borders of white and pastel stripe
- Cut 2 – 27" x 1" (+sa) borders of white and pastel stripe
- Sew 19" x 1" borders to top and bottom
- Sew 27" x 1" borders to sides
- Cut 2 – 27" x 3½" (+sa) borders of white and pastel print
- Cut 2 – 28" x 3½" (+sa) borders of white and pastel print
- Sew 27" x 3½" borders to sides
- Sew 28" x 3½" borders to top and bottom
- Quilt and bind

Diagram #1

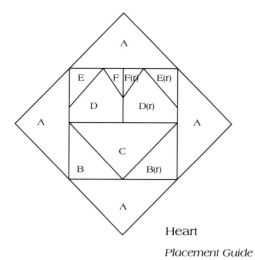

Heart

Placement Guide

Diagram #2

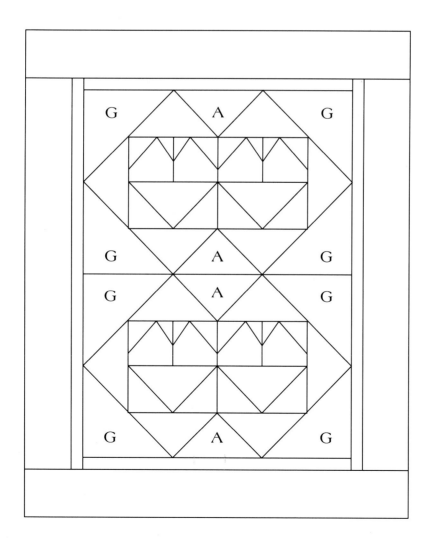

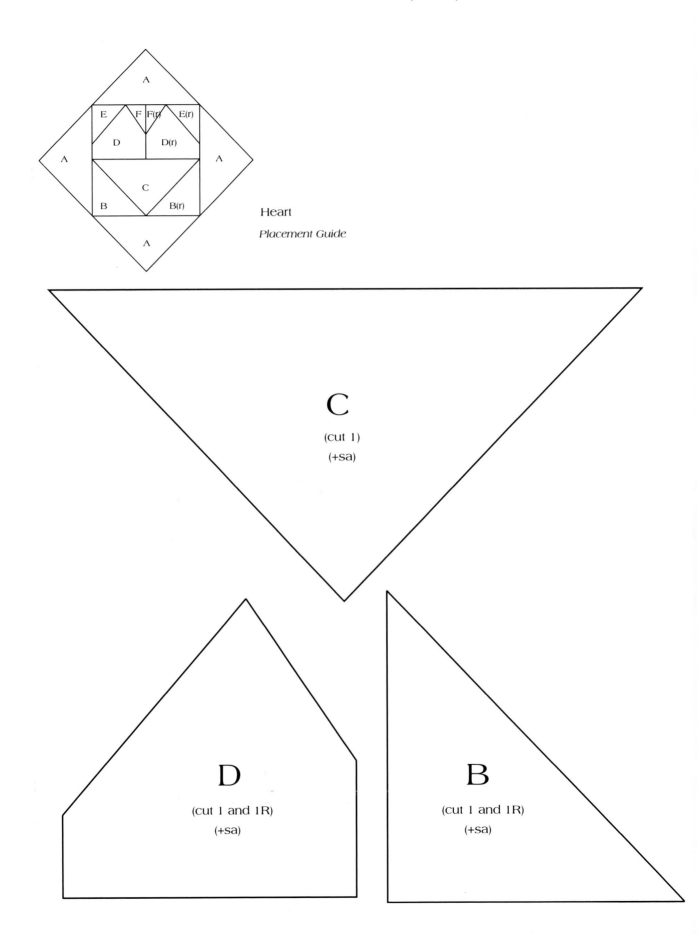

Heart

Placement Guide

C

(cut 1)

(+sa)

D

(cut 1 and 1R)

(+sa)

B

(cut 1 and 1R)

(+sa)

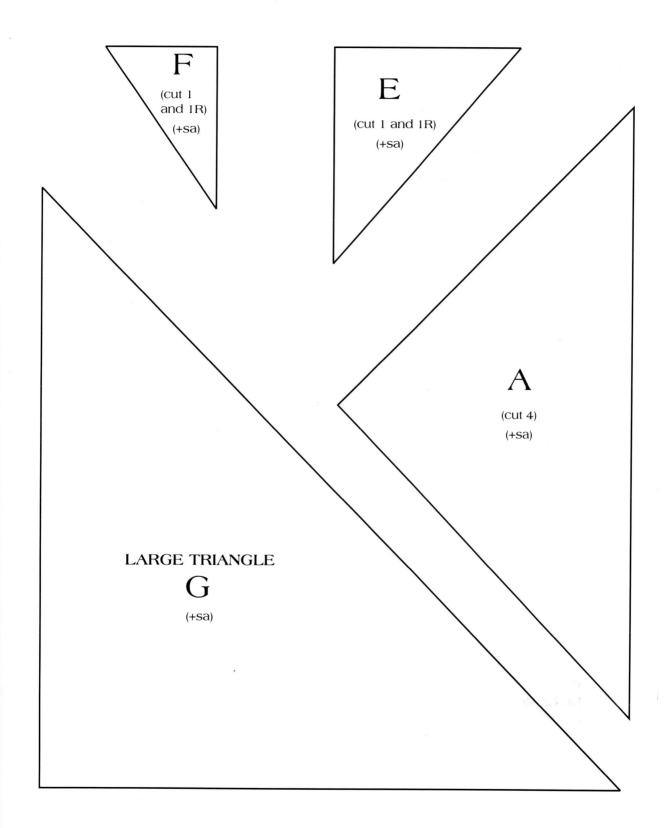

F
(cut 1
and 1R)
(+sa)

E
(cut 1 and 1R)
(+sa)

A
(cut 4)
(+sa)

LARGE TRIANGLE
G
(+sa)

EMPTY BASKETS
17.5" x 27.5" finished size

FABRIC REQUIREMENTS
¼ yd yellow for baskets
⅛ yd background for each basket
⅛ yd pink stripe for inside border
¼ yd for large border

INSTRUCTIONS (Patterns: pages 158-159)
- Cut 2 baskets – pieces C, E, Cr, 2H, J – of yellow floral
- Cut 1 background – pieces 2A, B, Br, D, Dr, F, 2G, I, K, Kr – of small white & pastel print
- Cut 1 background of white & pastel plaid
- Piecing sequence:
    B, C, D,
    E, F
    Dr, Cr, Br
    G, H, I, H, G
    K, J, Kr
- Sew A's to top and bottom
- Sew two basket blocks together, one on top of the other
- Cut 2 – 10" x ¾" (+sa) borders of pastel stripe
- Cut 1 – 21½" x ¾" (+sa) borders of pastel stripe

- Sew 10" x ¾" borders to top and bottom
- Sew 21½" x ¾" borders to sides
- Cut 2 – 21½" x 3" (+sa) borders of white & pastel print
- Cut 2 – 17½" x 3" (+sa) borders of white & pastel print
- Sew 21½" x 3" borders to sides
- Sew 17½" x 3" borders to top and bottom
- Quilt and bind

Full Quilt Diagram

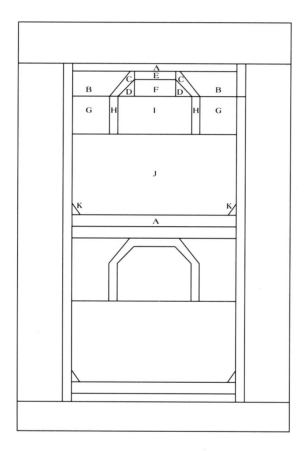

See Additional Patterns Section for these patterns:

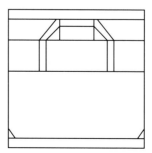

Page 158-159

BASKETS IN THE GARDEN
61.5" x 79" finished size

FABRIC REQUIREMENTS

    Light squares

      1 yd assorted pale pastels

    Dark squares

      1 yd assorted pinks (rose)

    Large basket

      ¼ yd yellow floral for basket

      ¼ yd white and pastel print for
      background

    Blue basket

      ⅛ yd blue plaid for basket

      ⅛ yd muslin for background

    Green basket

      ⅛ yd green print for basket

      ⅛ yd white and pastel print for
      background

    Small border

      ⅜ yd rose and cream stripe

    Large border

      1⅜ yd medium rose

    Binding

      ½ yd for straight binding

      ⅜ yd for bias binding

INSTRUCTIONS (Patterns: pages 138-139, 158-159,)

- Cut 3 large baskets (*Diagram #1*) - pieces C, E, Cr, 2H, J – of yellow floral
- Cut 3 large basket backgrounds (*Diagram #1*) - pieces 2A, B, Br, D, Dr, F, 2G, I, K,
  Kr of white and pastel print
- Piecing sequence for large baskets:

    B, C, D,

    E, F,

    Dr, Cr, Br

    GH, H, I, H, G,

    K, J, Kr

- Sew piece A to top and bottom
- Cut 3 green baskets (*Diagram #2*, Basket C) - pieces 2, 3 – of green print
- Cut 3 backgrounds (*Diagram #2*) – 1, 4, 4r, 5 – of white and pastel print
- Piecing sequence:

  Appliqué piece #2 onto piece #1

  4, 3, 4r

  5
- Cut 3 blue baskets (*Diagram #3*) – pieces 2, 3, 5 – of blue plaid
- Cut 3 backgrounds (*Diagram #3*) – pieces 1, 4, 4r, 6, 6r, 7 – of muslin
- Piecing sequence:

  Appliqué piece #2 onto piece #1

  4, 3, 4r

  6, 5, 6r

  7
- Cut 92 – 3½" (+sa) squares of dark pinks and roses
- Cut 91 – 3½" (+sa) squares of light pastels and white and pastel plaid
- Sew squares and baskets together as seen in *Diagram #4*

  (I sewed squares and baskets together in three sections as seen in *Diagram #5* and then sewed the sections together)
- Cut 2 – 45½" x 1½" (+sa) borders of rose and cream stripe
- Cut 2 – 66" x 1½" (+sa) borders of rose and cream stripe
- Sew 45½" x 1½" borders to top and bottom
- Sew 66" x 1½" borders to sides
- Cut 2 – 66" x 6½" (+sa) borders of rose
- Cut 2 – 61½" x 6½" (+sa) borders of rose
- Sew 66" x 6½" borders to sides
- Sew 61½" x 6½" borders to top and bottom

Diagram #1:
Large Basket

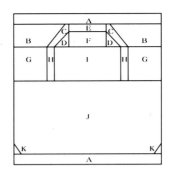

Diagram #3:
Small Basket

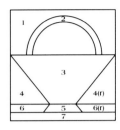

Page 158-159

Page 155

Below:
Diagram #2:
Basket C, templates

See Additional Patterns Section for the patterns above.

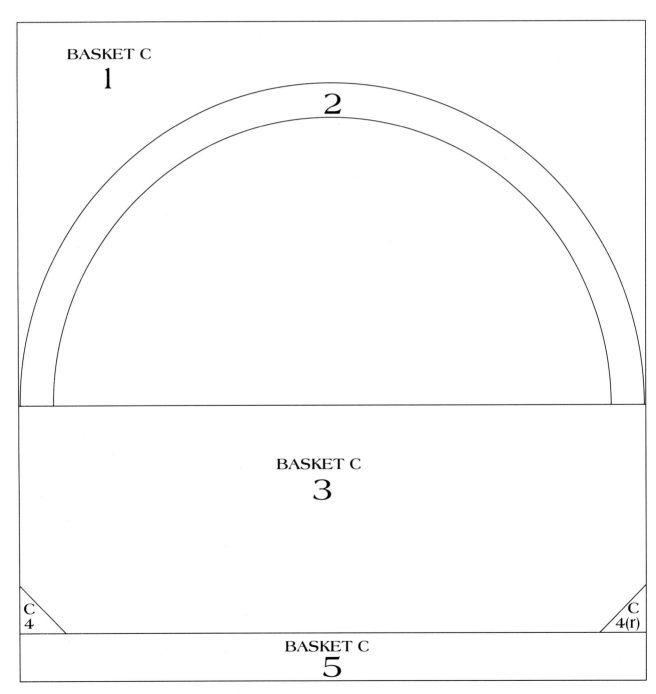

BASKET C
1

2

BASKET C
3

C
4

C
4(r)

BASKET C
5

Diagram #4

Diagram #5

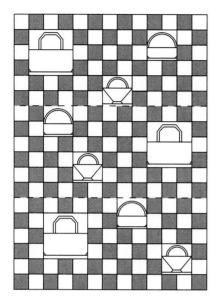

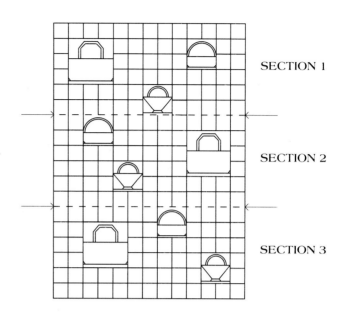

SECTION 1

SECTION 2

SECTION 3

3½" (+sa)

SQUARE

(cut 92 dark)
(cut 91 light)

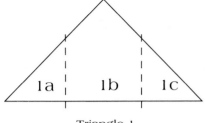

Triangle 1

Placement Guide

PATTERN:

SUMMER SKIES – page 42
LITTLE HOUSE – page 84

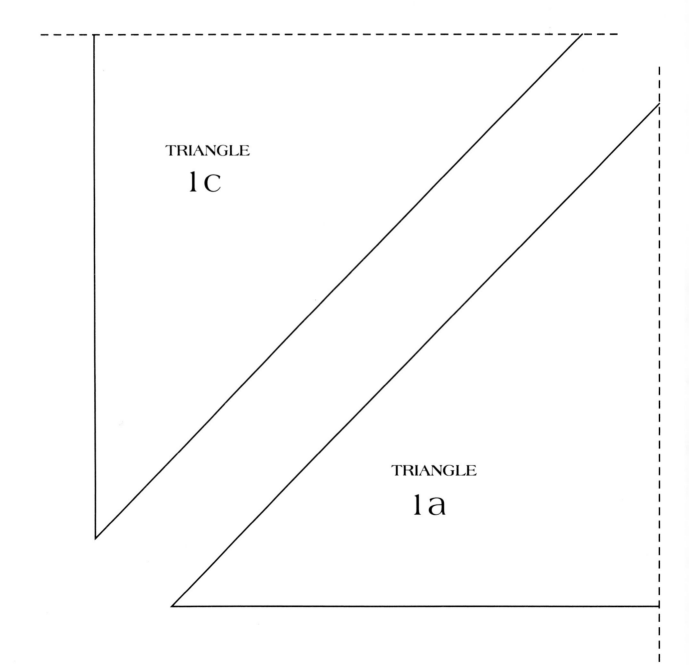

TRIANGLE
1C

TRIANGLE
1a

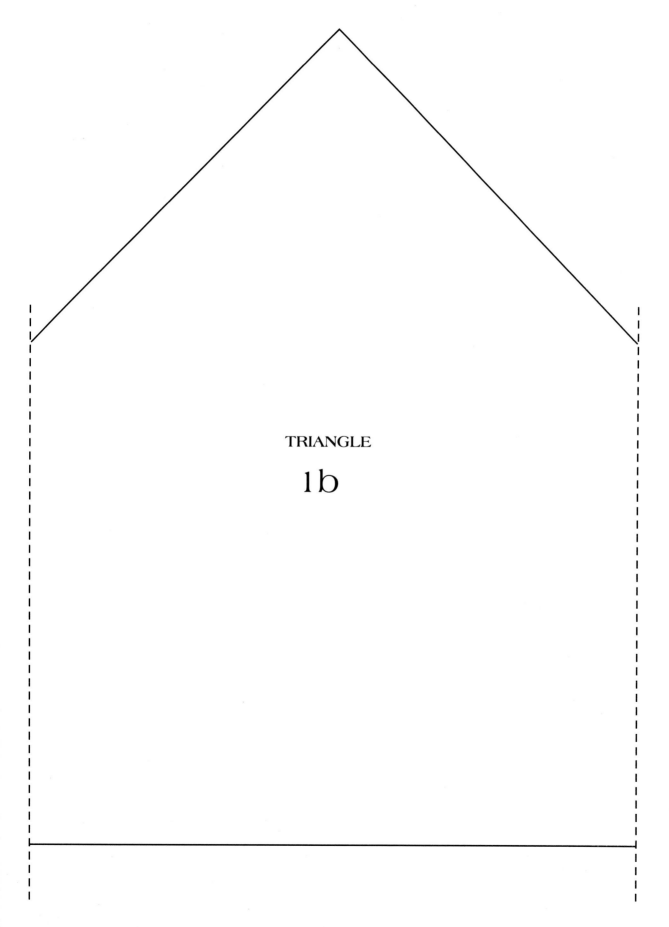

TRIANGLE

1b

PATTERN:

NEIGHBORS – page 74
LITTLE HOUSE – page 84

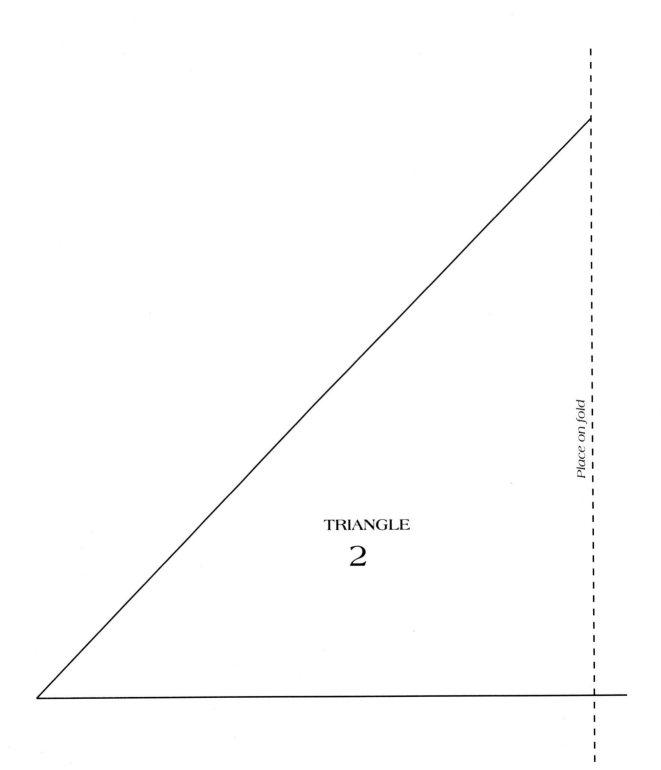

TRIANGLE

2

Place on fold

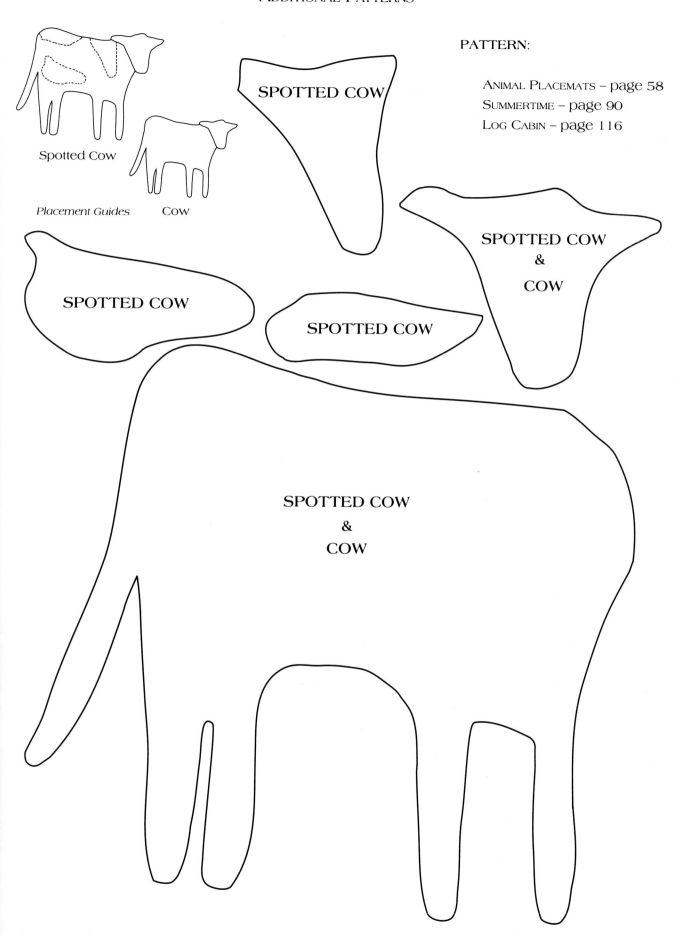

Spotted Cow

Placement Guides   Cow

SPOTTED COW

SPOTTED COW
&
COW

PATTERN:

ANIMAL PLACEMATS – page 58
SUMMERTIME – page 90
LOG CABIN – page 116

SPOTTED COW

SPOTTED COW

SPOTTED COW
&
COW

Blooming Tree

Placement Guide

PATTERN:

BLOOMING TREE

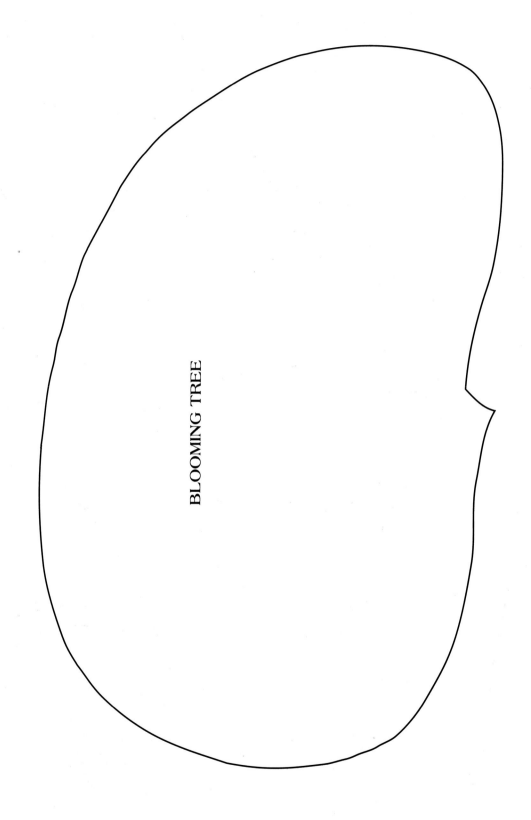

BLOOMING TREE

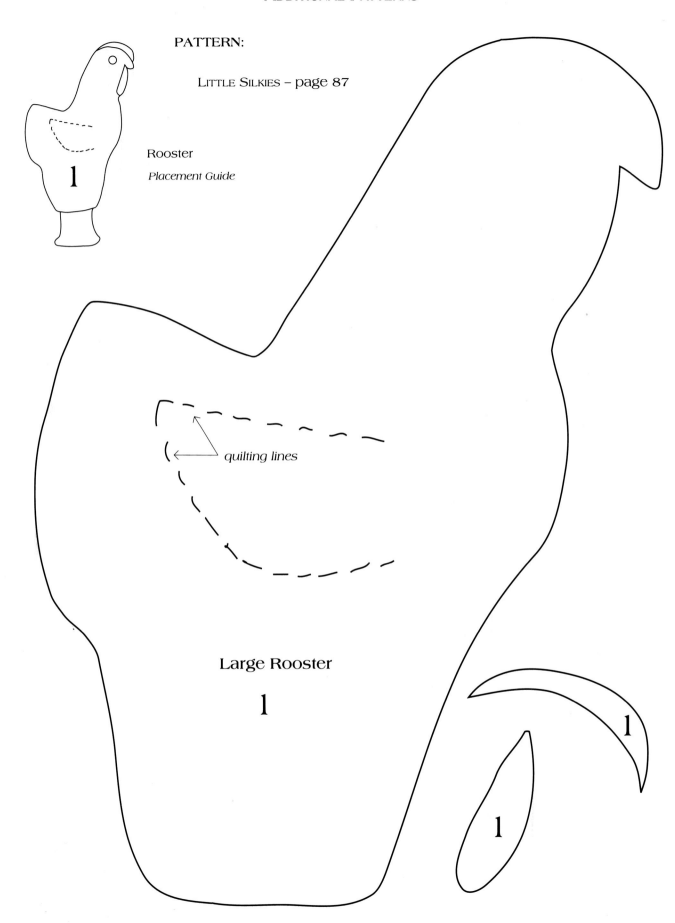

PATTERN:

LITTLE SILKIES – page 87

Rooster

Placement Guide

1

quilting lines

Large Rooster

1

1

1

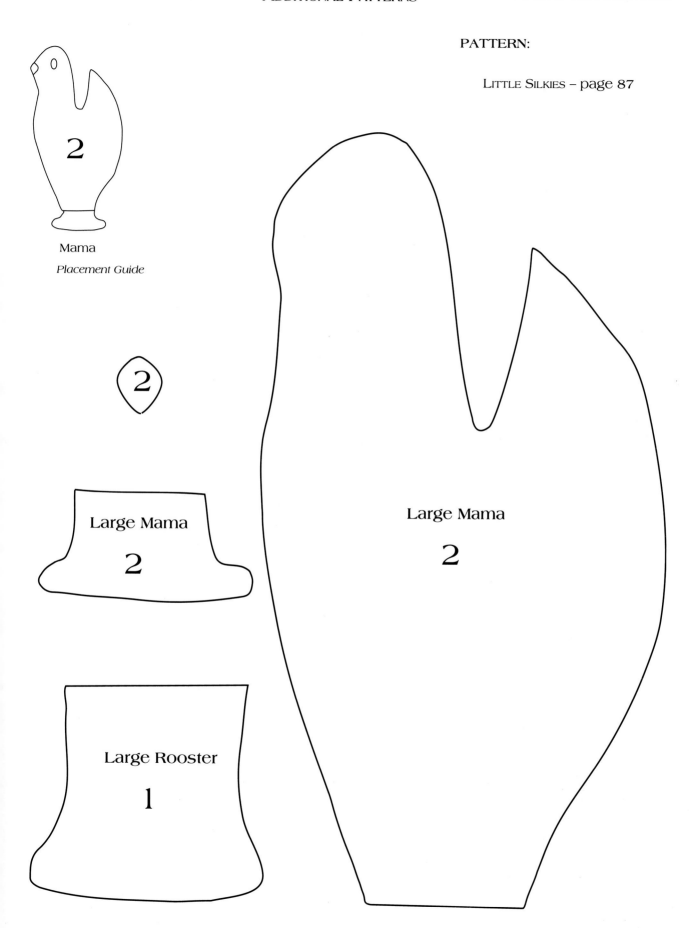

PATTERN:

LITTLE SILKIES – page 87

2

Mama

Placement Guide

2

Large Mama

2

Large Rooster

1

Large Mama

2

PATTERN:

LITTLE SILKIES – page 87

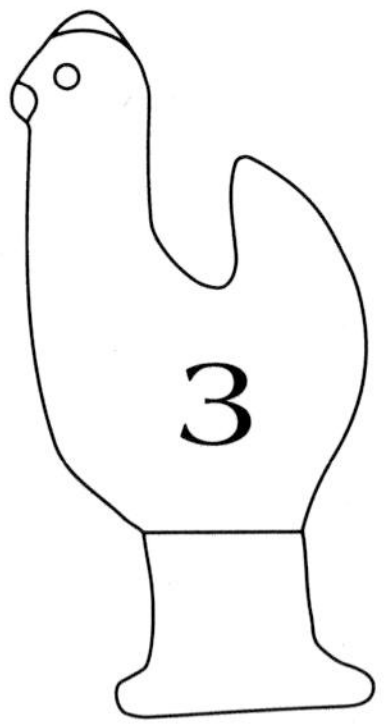

3

Junior

Placement Guide

3

3

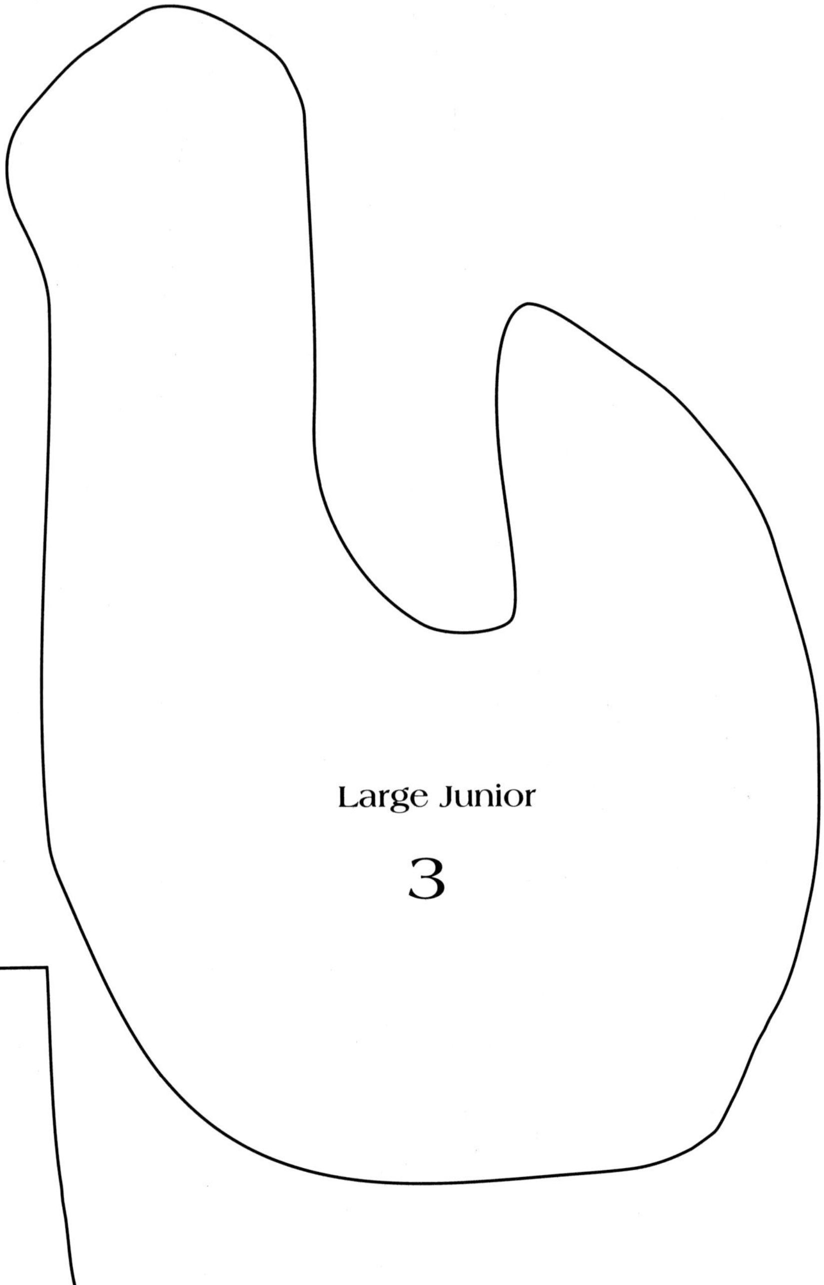

Large Junior

3

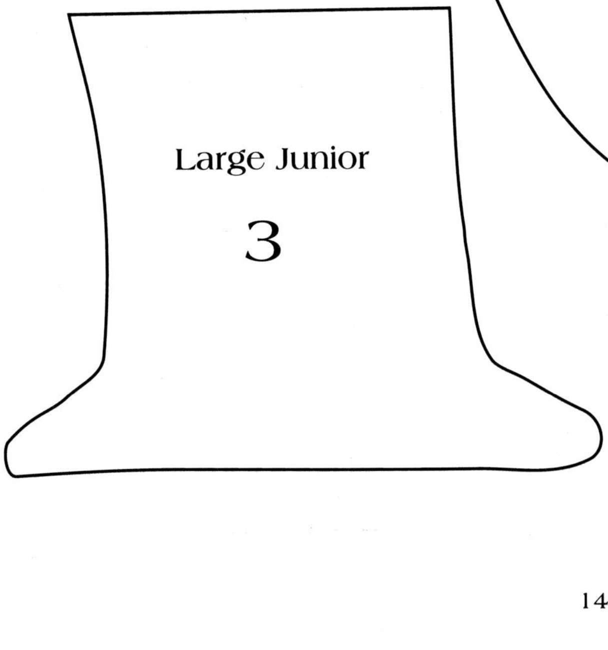

Large Junior

3

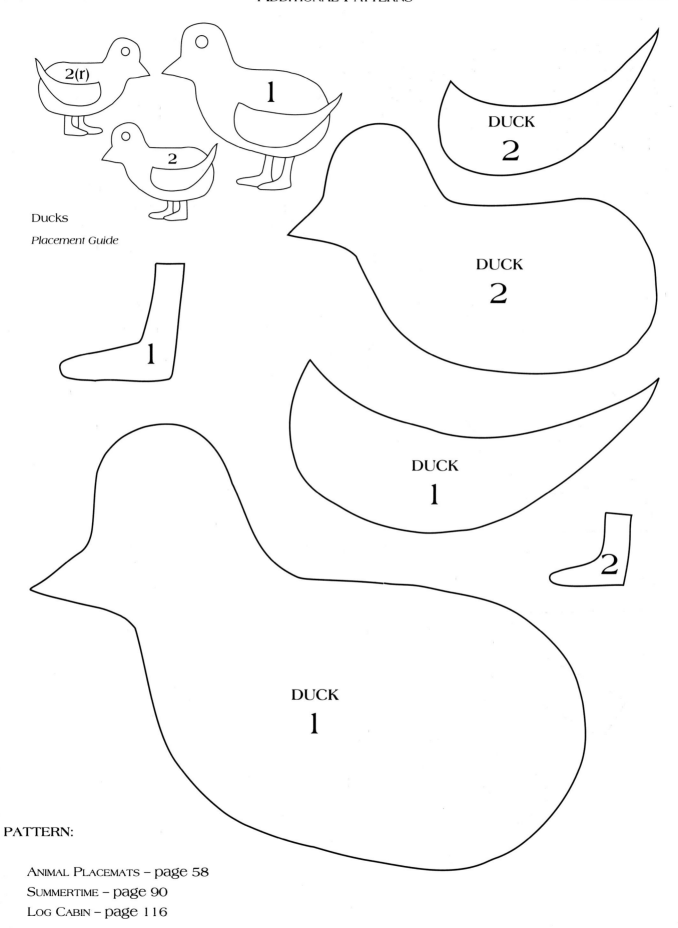

Ducks

Placement Guide

DUCK 2

DUCK 2

1

DUCK 1

2

DUCK 1

PATTERN:

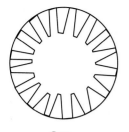

Sun

Placement Guide

PATTERN:

SUNNY DAYS – page 60
NEIGHBORS – page 74
LOG CABIN – page 116

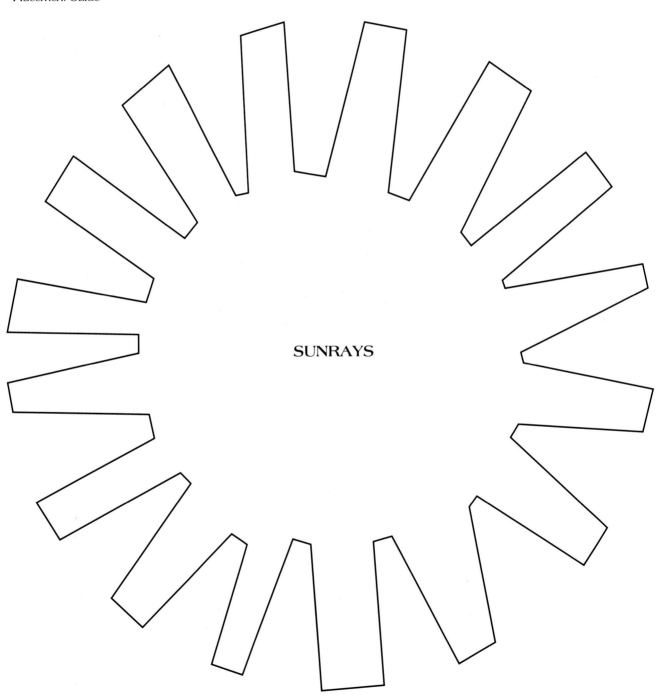

SUNRAYS

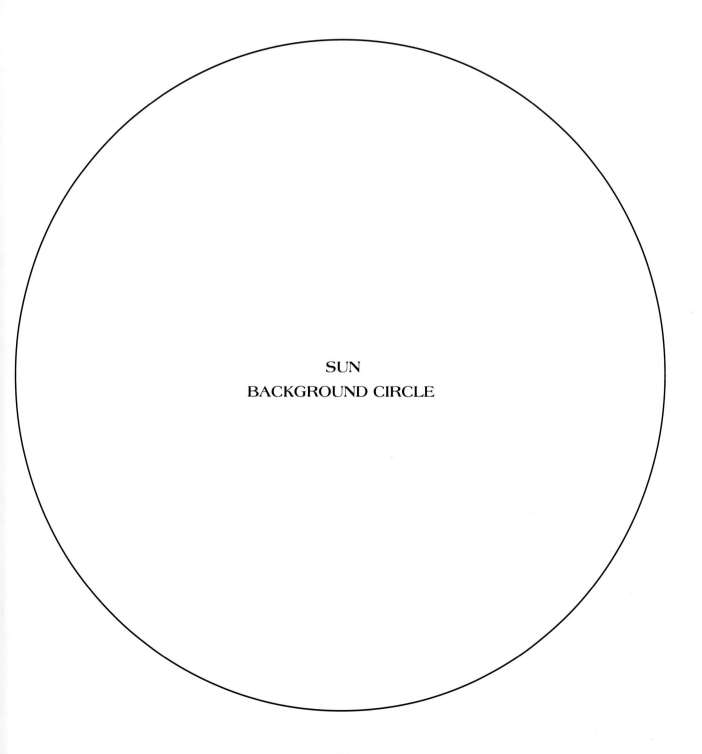

SUN
BACKGROUND CIRCLE

PATTERN:

NEIGHBORS – page 74
LITTLE HOUSE – page 84

House

Placement Guide

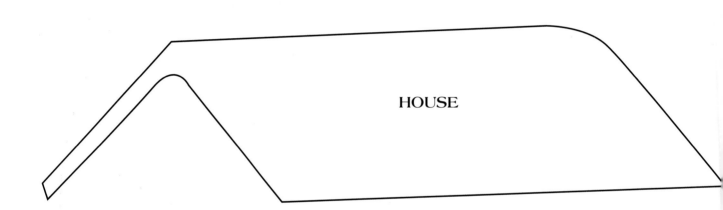

HOUSE

HOUSE

(cut 2)

HOUSE

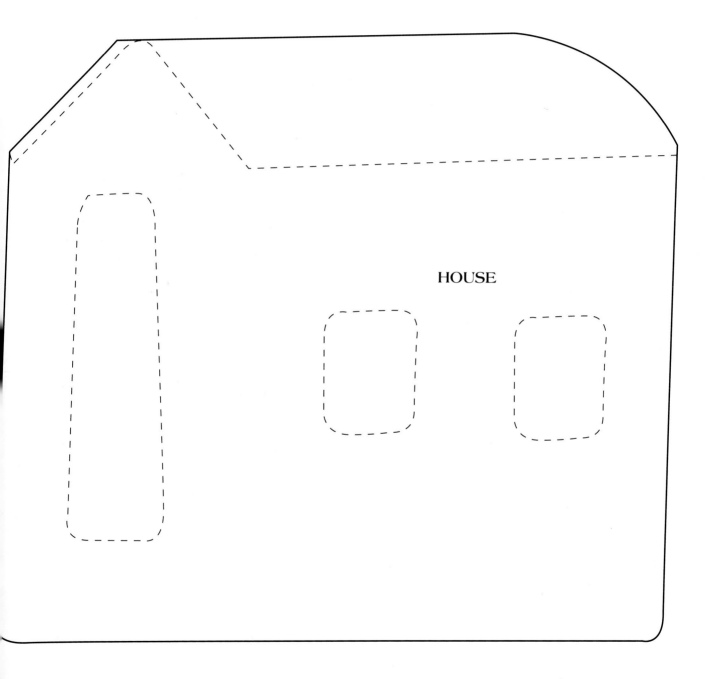

HOUSE

PATTERN:

NEIGHBORS – page 74
LOG CABIN – page 116

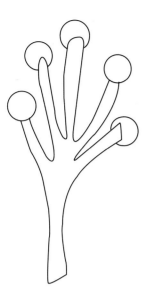

Cherry Tree

Placement Guide

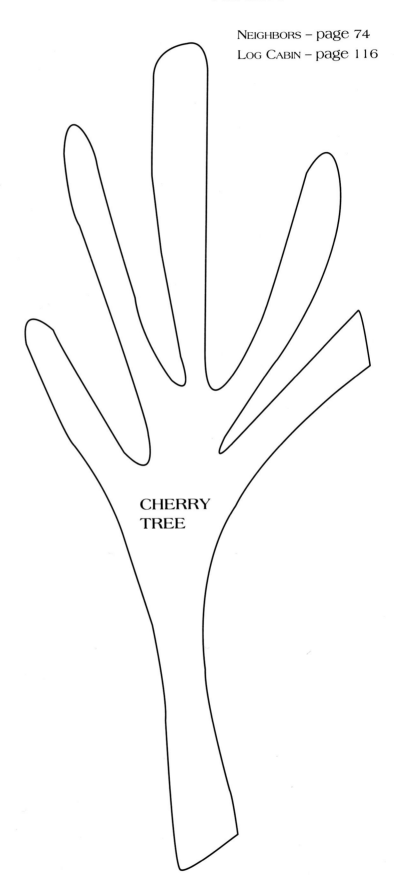

CHERRY
TREE

CHERRY
TREE
(cut 5)

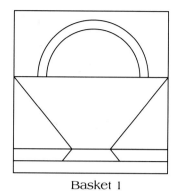

Basket 1

Placement Guide

PATTERN:

BASKETS & BERRIES – page 88
LOG CABIN – page 116
BASKETS IN GARDEN – page 136

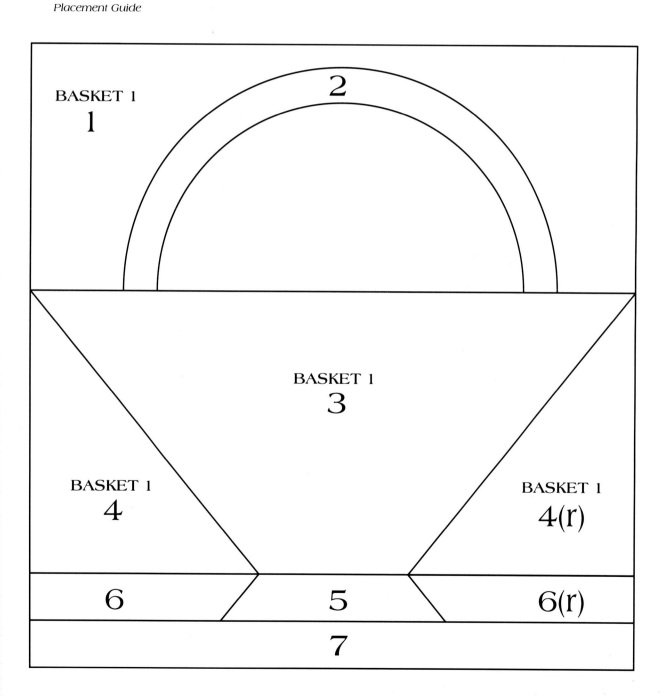

BASKET 1
1

2

BASKET 1
3

BASKET 1
4

BASKET 1
4(r)

6

5

6(r)

7

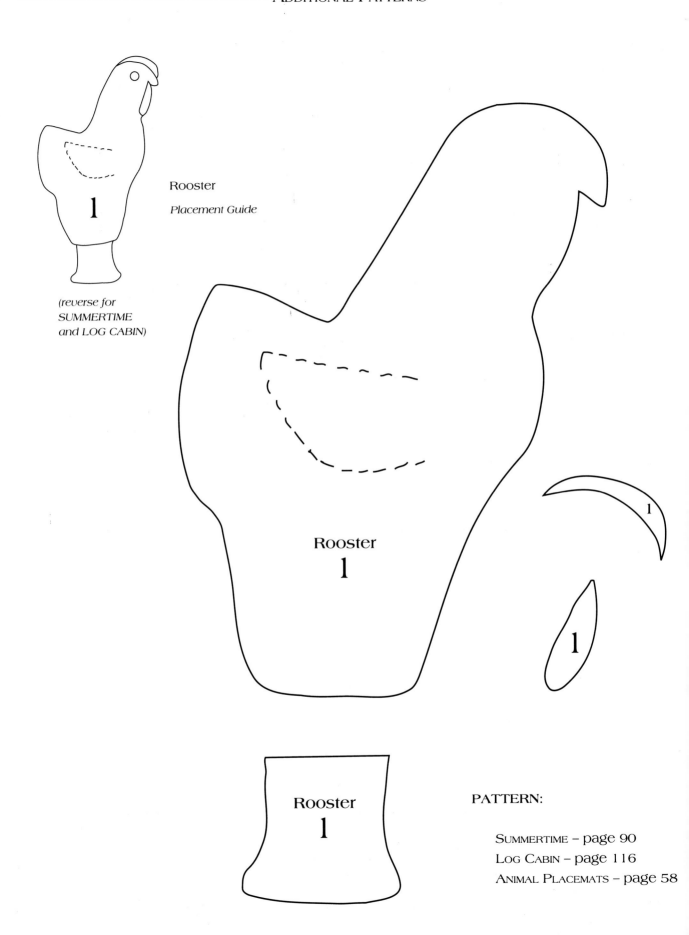

Rooster

Placement Guide

(reverse for SUMMERTIME and LOG CABIN)

1

Rooster
1

1

1

Rooster
1

PATTERN:

SUMMERTIME – page 90
LOG CABIN – page 116
ANIMAL PLACEMATS – page 58

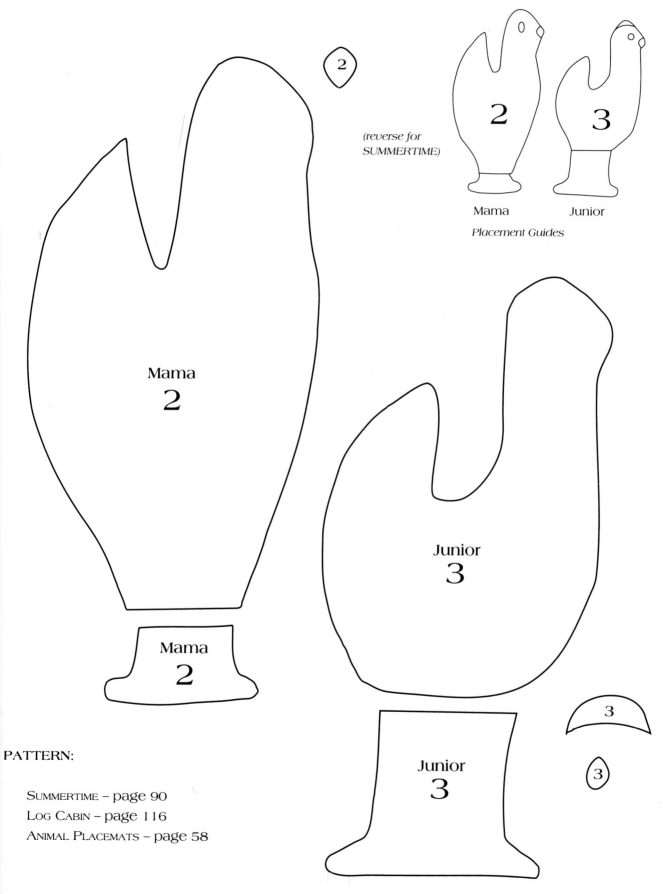

(reverse for
SUMMERTIME)

Mama

Junior

Placement Guides

2

Mama
2

Mama
2

Junior
3

Junior
3

3

3

PATTERN:

SUMMERTIME – page 90

LOG CABIN – page 116

ANIMAL PLACEMATS – page 58

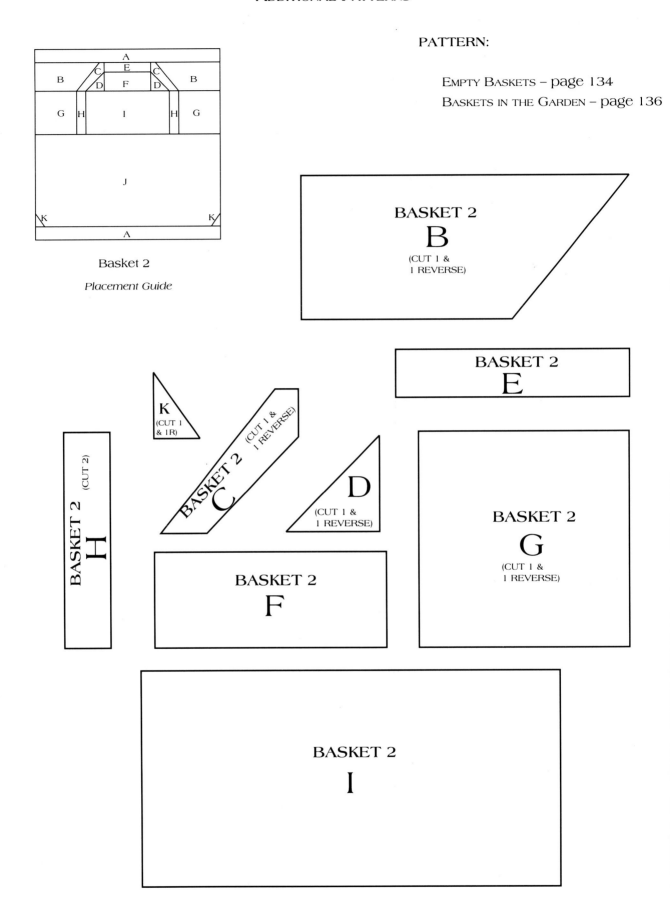

PATTERN:

EMPTY BASKETS – page 134

BASKETS IN THE GARDEN – page 136

Basket 2

Placement Guide

BASKET 2

B

(CUT 1 &
1 REVERSE)

BASKET 2

E

K

(CUT 1
& 1R)

BASKET 2

C

(CUT 1 &
1 REVERSE)

D

(CUT 1 &
1 REVERSE)

BASKET 2

H

(CUT 2)

BASKET 2

G

(CUT 1 &
1 REVERSE)

BASKET 2

F

BASKET 2

I

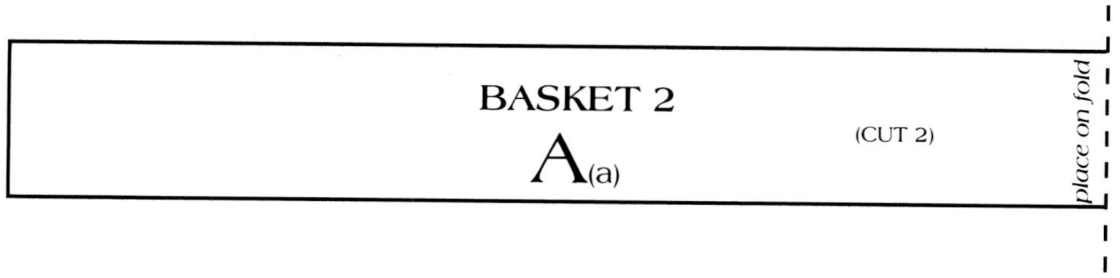

BASKET 2

A(a)

(CUT 2)

place on fold

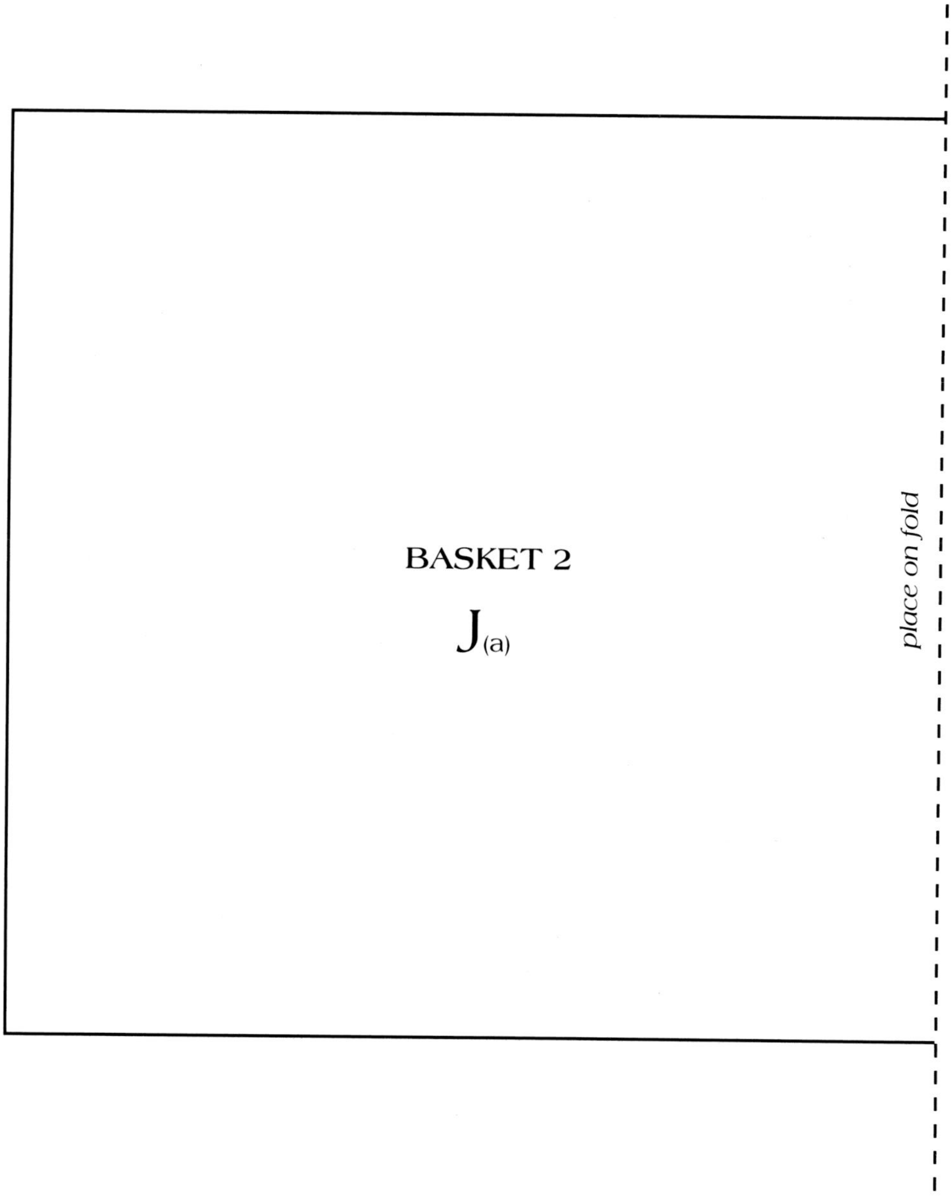

BASKET 2

J(a)

place on fold

∾American Quilter's Society∾

dedicated to publishing books for today's quilters

The following AQS publications are currently available:

- **Adapting Architectural Details for Quilts,** Carol Wagner, #2282: AQS, 1991, 88 pages, softbound, $12.95
- **American Beauties: Rose & Tulip Quilts,** Gwen Marston & Joe Cunningham, #1907: AQS, 1988, 96 pages, softbound, $14.95
- **America's Pictorial Quilts,** Caron L. Mosey, #1662: AQS, 1985, 112 pages, hardbound, $19.95
- **Applique Designs: My Mother Taught Me to Sew,** Faye Anderson, #2121: AQS, 1990, 80 pages, softbound, $12.95
- **Arkansas Quilts: Arkansas Warmth,** Arkansas Quilter's Guild, Inc., #1908: AQS, 1987, 144 pages, hardbound, $24.95
- **The Art of Hand Applique,** Laura Lee Fritz, #2122: AQS, 1990, 80 pages, softbound, $14.95
- **...Ask Helen More About Quilting Designs,** Helen Squire, #2099: AQS, 1990, 54 pages, 17 x 11, spiral-bound, $14.95
- **Award-Winning Quilts & Their Makers: Vol. I, The Best of AQS Shows – 1985-1987,** #2207: AQS, 1991, 232 pages, softbound, $24.95
- **Award-Winning Quilts & Their Makers: Vol. II, The Best of AQS Shows – 1988-1989,** #2354: AQS, 1992, 176 pages, softbound, $24.95
- **Award-Winning Quilts & Their Makers: Vol. III, The Best of AQS Shows – 1990-1991,** #3425: AQS, 1993, 180 pages, softbound, $24.95
- **Classic Basket Quilts,** Elizabeth Porter & Marianne Fons, #2208: AQS, 1991, 128 pages, softbound, $16.95
- **A Collection of Favorite Quilts,** Judy Florence, #2119: AQS, 1990, 136 pages, softbound, $18.95
- **Creative Machine Art,** Sharee Dawn Roberts, #2355: AQS, 1992, 142 pages, 9 x 9, softbound, $24.95
- **Dear Helen, Can You Tell Me?...all about quilting designs,** Helen Squire, #1820: AQS, 1987, 51 pages, 17 x 11, spiral-bound, $12.95
- **Dye Painting!,** Ann Johnston, #3399: AQS, 1992, 88 pages, softbound, $19.95
- **Dyeing & Overdyeing of Cotton Fabrics,** Judy Mercer Tescher, #2030: AQS, 1990, 54 pages, softbound, $9.95
- **Flavor Quilts for Kids to Make: Complete Instructions for Teaching Children to Dye, Decorate & Sew Quilts,** Jennifer Amor #2356: AQS, 1991, 120 pages, softbound, $12.95
- **From Basics to Binding: A Complete Guide to Making Quilts,** Karen Kay Buckley, #2381: AQS, 1992, 160 pages, softbound, $16.95
- **Fun & Fancy Machine Quiltmaking,** Lois Smith, #1982: AQS, 1989, 144 pages, softbound, $19.95
- **Gallery of American Quilts 1830-1991: Book III,** #3421: AQS, 1992, 128 pages, softbound, $19.95
- **The Grand Finale: A Quilter's Guide to Finishing Projects,** Linda Denner, #1924: AQS, 1988, 96 pages, softbound, $14.95
- **Heirloom Miniatures,** Tina M. Gravatt, #2097: AQS, 1990, 64 pages, softbound, $9.95
- **Infinite Stars,** Gayle Bong, #2283: AQS, 1992, 72 pages, softbound, $12.95
- **The Ins and Outs: Perfecting the Quilting Stitch,** Patricia J. Morris, #2120: AQS, 1990, 96 pages, softbound, $9.95
- **Irish Chain Quilts: A Workbook of Irish Chains & Related Patterns,** Joyce B. Peaden, #1906: AQS, 1988, 96 pages, softbound, $14.95
- **The Log Cabin Returns to Kentucky: Quilts from the Pilgrim/Roy Collection,** Gerald Roy and Paul Pilgrim, #3329: AQS, 1992, 36 pages, 9 x 7, softbound, $12.95
- **Marbling Fabrics for Quilts: A Guide for Learning & Teaching,** Kathy Fawcett & Carol Shoaf, #2206: AQS, 1991, 72 pages, softbound, $12.95
- **More Projects and Patterns: A Second Collection of Favorite Quilts,** Judy Florence, #3330: AQS, 1992, 152 pages, softbound, $18.95
- **Nancy Crow: Quilts and Influences,** Nancy Crow, #1981: AQS, 1990, 256 pages, 9 x 12, hardcover, $29.95
- **Nancy Crow: Work in Transition,** Nancy Crow, #3331: AQS, 1992, 32 pages, 9 x 10, softbound, $12.95
- **New Jersey Quilts – 1777 to 1950: Contributions to an American Tradition,** The Heritage Quilt Project of New Jersey; text by Rachel Cochran, Rita Erickson, Natalie Hart & Barbara Schaffer, #3332: AQS, 1992, 256 pages, softbound, $29.95
- **No Dragons on My Quilt,** Jean Ray Laury with Ritva Laury & Lizabeth Laury, #2153: AQS, 1990, 52 pages, hardcover, $12.95
- **Oklahoma Heritage Quilts,** Oklahoma Quilt Heritage Project #2032: AQS, 1990, 144 pages, softbound, $19.95
- **Old Favorites in Miniature,** Tina Gravatt, #3469: AQS, 1993, 104 pages, softbound, $15.95
- **Quilt Groups Today: Who They Are, Where They Meet, What They Do, and How to Contact Them; A Complete Guide for 1992-1993,** #3308: AQS, 1992, 336 pages, softbound, $14.95
- **Quilting Patterns from Native American Designs,** Dr. Joyce Mori, #3467: AQS, 1993, 80 pages, softbound, $12.95
- **Quilting with Style: Principles for Great Pattern Design,** Gwen Marston & Joe Cunningham, #3470: AQS, 1993, 192 pages, 9 x 12, hardcover, $24.95
- **Quiltmaker's Guide: Basics & Beyond,** Carol Doak, #2284: AQS, 1992, 208 pages, softbound, $19.95
- **Quilts: Old & New, A Similar View,** Paul D. Pilgrim and Gerald E. Roy, #3715: AQS, 1993, 40 pages, softbound, $12.95
- **Quilts: The Permanent Collection – MAQS,** #2257: AQS, 1991, 100 pages, 10 x 6½, softbound, $9.95
- **Sensational Scrap Quilts,** Darra Duffy Williamson, #2357: AQS, 1992, 152 pages, softbound, $24.95
- **Show Me Helen...How to Use Quilting Designs,** Helen Squire, #3375: AQS, 1993, 155 pages, softbound, $15.95
- **Sets & Borders,** Gwen Marston & Joe Cunningham, #1821: AQS, 1987, 104 pages, softbound, $14.95
- **Somewhere in Between: Quilts and Quilters of Illinois,** Rita Barrow Barber, #1790: AQS, 1986, 78 pages, softbound, $14.95
- **Stenciled Quilts for Christmas,** Marie Monteith Sturmer, #2098: AQS, 1990, 104 pages, softbound, $14.95
- **A Treasury of Quilting Designs,** Linda Goodmon Emery, #2029: AQS, 1990, 80 pages, 14 x 11, spiral-bound, $14.95
- **Wonderful Wearables: A Celebration of Creative Clothing,** Virginia Avery, #2286: AQS, 1991, 184 pages, softbound, $24.95

These books can be found in local bookstores and quilt shops. If you are unable to locate a title in your area, you can order by mail from AQS, P.O. Box 3290, Paducah, KY 42002-3290. Please add $1 for the first book and 40¢ for each additional one to cover postage and handling. (International orders please add $1.50 for the first book and $1 for each additional one.)